THE ROLE
OF COMPUTERS
IN RELIGIOUS
EDUCATION

Kenneth B. Bedell

ABINGDON PRESS
NASHVILLE

THE ROLE OF COMPUTERS IN RELIGIOUS EDUCATION

This book is printed on acid-free paper.

Library of Congress Cataloging in Publication Data

BEDELL, KENNETH B.
  Role of computers in religious education.
  1. Christian education—Data processing.
  I. Title.
  BV1536.4.B44   1986   207   85-28653
        ISBN 0-687-36540-6 (alk. paper)

The computer game on pp. 77-81 is reprinted from *Creative Computing
Press* (August 1982), Copyright © 1982 Ahl Computing, Inc.

MANUFACTURED BY THE PARTHENON PRESS AT
NASHVILLE, TENNESSEE, UNITED STATES OF AMERICA

To
Elizabeth

CONTENTS

CHAPTER FOUR

CHAPTER FIVE

CHAPTER SIX

ACKNOWLEDGMENTS

T HIS book owes much to the students and participants in courses and workshops on church computing which I have conducted over the past two years.
They have indulged my comment that religious education is
the sleeping giant in the church computer revolution, and
many have shared their own experiences with attempts to
use computers for religious education.

Several people deserve special thanks for their help.
Robin Gohn of York, Pennsylvania, who works with
churches to help them implement computer-assisted
education programs, shared her collection of religious
education software with me. Dr. James Eastman, manager
of Churchwide EDP for the Presbyterian Church (U.S.A.),
discussed the project with me, suggested resources, and
prepared the Appendix. Dr. Leo Rigsby, chair of the
Department of Sociology at Temple University, read most
of the manuscript and offered helpful suggestions. Louise
Henry and Parker Rossman also read portions of the
manuscript. And Norman E. Anderson, librarian at
Gordon Conwell Theological Seminary, provided helpful
bibliographical material.

Kathie, Charity, and Sarah often complained because the
computer used to write this book was on a table in the room
they call their living room. But I know, as they do, that it
would have been impossible for me to complete this project
without their help and support.

CHAPTER ONE

ENTERING THE COMPUTER AGE

THE use of computers for education has excited the imagination of professional educators and computer enthusiasts for several years. Some religious educators have also been enchanted by the possibilities offered by this new technology. Initial experiments in the use of computers for religious education have included software programs to help children learn Bible names and books, computer games which can be played in a church school setting, and curriculum which takes advantage of computer-assisted instruction.

Before computers can be successfully integrated into the educational ministry of the church, however, it will be necessary to synthesize the skills of the computer programmer, the artistry of the educational design personnel, and the sensitivity of the theologians.

Dreamers can easily be carried away. Imagine religious education that catches a sense of excitement. Can the computer captivate and motivate children to learn? As more is discovered about the way children learn and respond, can a computer actually make church school exciting for children? Or imagine programs of religious education in which adults, as well as children, can learn more efficiently.

Have computers arrived just in time? In an age when the average congregation is almost biblically illiterate and knows even less about traditions of the church, will the computer make it possible to convey religious information so that people are better equipped to apply religion to daily life? Imagine a congregation that is not limited by geography, size, culture, or history because it has immediate access to a computerized library. Can computers universalize knowledge and information so that each individual has access to the best answer for every question? Could large computerized databases of religious information be available to every church school teacher, so that every question can be seriously investigated? Can computer-based communication systems make it possible for individuals to share and grow in new ways?

While the dreamers hope for excitement, more efficient learning, and better information flow, others wonder about the wisdom of trying to use computers for religious education. Ultimately, their questions must intertwine with fundamental questions about the purpose and methods of religious education.

The Purpose of This Book

This book is being written at a time when there are very limited resources for the religious educator eager to use computers. Computer equipment is too expensive to justify universal experimentation or trivial use. The mid-1980s are a time for planning, reflection, and experimentation. Early successes in the field can be exploited.

Because churches' administrative use of computers is more advanced than their educational application, there may be lessons religious educators can learn from church administrators. At the 1984 annual meeting of the Church Computer Users Network, James Eastman, the manager of Churchwide Electronic Data Processing Coordination for the Presbyterian Church (U.S.A.), stated that an important side effect of the introduction of computers into church offices is that churches are asking important questions about what they are trying to accomplish and how their office practices relate to the mission of the church. "This is bringing a renewal to churches even when they decide not to use a computer." Religious education may benefit in the same way. It may be that the most important contribution of considering the use of computers will be a renewal of religious education.

If this book helps with the process of evaluating computers for religious education, it has accomplished its purpose, even if the evaluation process results in the decision that computers are inappropriate for a particular congregation. The purpose is not to convince people that they need computers. It is hoped, rather, that as a result of investigating computers, there will be an improvement in the quality of religious education, whether or not computers are used.

One use of computers will be in the administration of religious education programs. Here the experience of church administrators will be directly applicable. These issues are discussed in Chapter 7. But the potential contribution of computers is not limited to administration. This book would never have been written if the author did not suspect that in some cases today, and in many more cases in the near future, computers will offer the potential for a positive contribution to religious education. But the process of evaluating computers is seen as valuable, even though they will not be used immediately.

For instance, a congregation might look at the possibility of spending $10,000 on computer equipment; in the midst of the consideration, the congregation's limited resources for religious education might be exposed, so the church might decide to invest instead in chalkboards and cassette recorders. In another case, the investigation of computers could result in the observation that before computers could be used effectively, there would need to be extensive training of the church school staff. But rather than begin to learn about a new technology, the teachers might decide to build on the skills they already have and spend time in extensive training with more traditional methods.

In both these situations the decision would be to postpone the introduction of computers into the church school classroom. But the more important consequence would be improvement in the quality of religious education.

The first step in evaluating computers is to clarify the goals and purposes of religious education. Chapter 4 examines the possible ways computers can be used in church school classrooms, but it would be impossible to begin using computers without first clarifying the goals of classroom religious education. Chapter 5 looks beyond the church school to consider ways computers can be used for religious education in the home and community. As one possibility, the church could become an information provider. Again, issues of the appropriate role for religious education are obvious. A library is central in the life of a university or seminary. But what is the place of an information center in a church? While this question is not specifically a computer question, the introduction of computers gives us a framework for its consideration.

Chapter 6 looks at some ways computers can be part of curriculum development by having people in the church write software at their computer club meetings. But no church could consider such a project without first dealing with the broader issues of the appropriate content for a religious education program and how it is to be defined. The recent intrusion of computers into the educational scene demands a reevaluation of the complicated questions surrounding the relationship of culture, technology, and religion.

Marshall McLuhan has argued that the medium of cultural transmission itself contains a message that cannot be contradicted by the content of the media. McLuhan believes that books, television, and computers say something about the nature of reality. When people use a particular medium in education, they convey a message about ultimate reality. This argument implies that technology itself can transmit religious values.

An opposing argument is that computers (or television or books) are only tools for the transmission of information, culture, or religious ideas. They can be used for good or evil, just as a knife is a tool that can be used for good or evil. But are computers really value free? This question, discussed in Chapter 8, can most profitably be considered after the possible uses of computers in religious education have been examined.

In this introduction a more trivial question is considered: Can we introduce new educational techniques into churches without first examining the goals of our religious education programs? The answer to this question is no. But there is no clear consensus about the exact goals of religious education.

The approach each of us takes toward religious education is determined by our understanding of God and ultimate reality. Yet the sad fact is that there often is a discontinuity between the faith we express and our practice in religious education. At times this is due to inattention—the contradictions between beliefs and educational practices are not noticed. At other times the resources available to us introduce the contradictions.

As computers enter religious education, it is important to pay close attention not only to how they are being used but also to what is implied in the way we choose to use them. The individual teachers evaluating computer software, the church committee looking into the purchase of computer equipment, the denomination struggling with the question of whether to publish educational software–all must first clearly define their approach to religious education. The expense of using computers is sufficient reason to discourage inattention to the implications of teaching methods or resources.

Theoretical Approaches to Religious Education

This book is designed to be of assistance to anyone considering the use of computers for religious education, regardless of the theoretical approach. Harold Burgess, in *An Invitation to Religious Education,* has described four common approaches. Each approach is briefly summarized below, and questions raised by the introduction of computers are suggested. While no individual, congregation, or denomination will neatly fall into one of the categories listed by Burgess, his topology offers a framework for the first task in evaluating potential computer use:

formulating a clear statement of the goals and purposes of religious education.

Burgess calls the first approach to religious education the traditional theological theoretical approach. This approach is primarily concerned with the communication of a divine message and focuses on the transmission of this message of salvation, which has been received by revelation. The teacher must first have received this message and be called to faithfully transmit it to the students, who will benefit not only from the knowledge that is transmitted but by receiving eternal life. This approach lends itself easily to preaching or lecture as the educational method, and to the use of catechisms.

A computer is of particular interest to those who follow this approach. They believe that the content of religious education is of primary importance but that teachers may misunderstand or misrepresent the message. Because a computer must be exactly programmed, it will always present information in the same way, and since it is a machine, the message cannot be corrupted by the sins of the teacher.

For example, those who follow the traditional theological approach might use drill-and-practice exercises in which the computer asks questions and checks for accurate responses. Since the computer will never tire, the student can be drilled until the accepted answer is always given.

But the very fact that a computer is a machine presents the greatest problem to those who take a traditional theological theoretical approach. As Burgess observes, both the Roman Catholic and the Protestant traditional theorists "typically hold that, over and above any use of teaching method, the teacher's personal life and Christian witness is foundational to religious teaching success."[1] Can a computer ever participate in religious education, since it cannot itself comprehend the meaning of the divinely revealed message?

The second approach discussed by Burgess is the social-cultural theoretical. This approach views the Bible as a resource in the process of raising social consciousness and focuses on the individual and the society, rather than on the divinely sent message. The goal is not the salvation of the student, but that the student may become a constructive contributor to society. This approach owes much to the philosophy of John Dewey. Burgess points out that

> Dewey's theoretical and practical notions significantly affected the development of the social-cultural theoretical approach to religious education through the integration of his philosophical, moral, and educational ideas into the professional training programs and literature of the so-called religious educational movement, especially during the earlier decades of the twentieth century.[2]

Representatives of this approach criticized dogmatic statements of religion and called for experiential learning, using a scientific approach. Religious educators influenced by Dewey encourage self-direction by students, discourage punishment, attempt to tailor instruction to the student, and move educational activity beyond the classroom.

Adherents to the social-cultural approach to religious education welcome the introduction of a computer, so that the student can more fully participate in defining the learnings. They applaud the evidence that computers increase the involvement of students and motivate by capturing the students' attention.

This approach might use computers in a variety of ways. Programs of education could be tailored to each student. Because the computer can use large amounts of information, there can be many areas of content from which an individual student can choose. Even at an early age, students could use computers to aid in individual research and discovery.

But computers also present a very serious problem for these people. As used in education today, computers do not allow for a growing and changing situation. The very nature of the computer requires that educational materials be carefully structured. Computers provide an experience that is deterministic. So the religious educator who has adopted the social-cultural approach must ask: Can a computer which provides a student with a structured experience of reality assist with religious education, when the purpose of religious education is to provide the student with skills to participate in an ever changing, growing, and maturing social setting?

Burgess has more difficulty in clearly defining the third approach—the contemporary theological theoretical. The spokespeople for this view represent a wide range of theological and educational commitments. He says:

> However, these theorists appear to be essentially united in (1) their opposition to the optimistic brand of liberal theology espoused by social-cultural theorists, (2) their recognition that man is in need of redemption, and (3) their commitment to the position that the Christian community is the locus of religious life and education. In addition, some form of participatory relationship in the community of Christians is a usual feature of the religious education practices advocated by contemporary theological theorists.[3]

The major distinction between the traditional and contemporary theological approaches is the way each understands the role of the church. The traditional approach views the traditions of the church as a source of the revealed message of God and believes that the church is responsible for faithfully transmitting that message, whereas the contemporary theological approach views the church as the context wherein faith development can occur. Adherents to this approach think that religious education is not learning about God, but learning how to be part of a community of faith. Spiritual growth and salvation are found by participation in the church, not because particular revealed truths are appropriated.

The contemporary theological approach is distinguished from the social-cultural approach not only by its interest in assisting the student to discover the way to salvation, but also in its focus on the church rather than on society. But the contemporary theological shares with the social-cultural a rejection of the possibility of formulating clear dogmatic statements which can be transferred through the religious education process. For the contemporary approach, the purpose of religious education is to provide each student with experience and skills which will foster participation in a community of faith, where religious understanding is formulated, tested, and supported.

At first it may seem that the individualized nature of human/computer interaction would present an insurmountable problem for religious educators who subscribe to the contemporary theological approach. How can a computer, which isolates individuals, contribute to religious education, if the purpose of religious education is to develop the skills of participating in a community of faith? But advocates of the contemporary theological approach have already discovered two ways to use computers, and they may find many more. A computer is used as the center of a group activity, for stimulation; it is also used to store messages and information—it becomes a large message board designed to support communication and participation in a community.

Burgess' fourth approach to religious education is the social-science theoretical. This is the approach advocated by James Michael Lee. Lee has written three books, each with the subtitle *A Social-Science Approach.*[4] For Lee, the practice of religious education is subservient to specific aims. According to Burgess, there are four:

> first, the modification of the student's cognitive behavior so that he has command of religious knowledge and understandings by which he is able to intelligently synthesize his faith; second, the modification of the student's effective behavior so that he acquires the capacity to form Christian values, attitudes, etc. . . . ; third, the modification of the student's product behavior so that he has command of existential, theological, and other relevant subject matter; and fourth, the modification of the student's process behavior so that he can ongoingly think, feel, and act in a continuingly relevant Christian way.[5]

The social-science approach takes very seriously the empirical studies of effectiveness of various educational methods. Lee does not consider teaching methods to be value free: The proper content of religious education is the religious instruction act itself. In fact, the social-science approach distinguishes itself from other approaches because it denies the duality of method and content. This does not imply that there is only one method of religious education, because the content cannot be defined simplistically. Lee suggests eight levels of content for religious education: product content, process content, cognitive content, effective content, verbal content, nonverbal content, unconscious content, and life-style content. The consideration of a particular method of teaching must begin by identifying the content before the method can be evaluated.

The teacher is viewed not as a model of Christian life, but rather as a technician, judged by the success or failure of applying the craft of religious education. The moral character and the spiritual development of the teacher are not as important as the ability to apply sound educational principles to ensure that the desired objectives are achieved. This does not mean that the personality of the teacher is of no consequence; it may be that personality is an important ingredient in the effectiveness of a particular teacher.

Those who advocate the social-science approach will eagerly study possible computer usage. The first question they will ask is whether there is empirical scientific evidence that computers can make any contribution to the effectiveness of teachers who have clear learning goals. If there is a positive response, then they will ask: Can computer-assisted instruction provide trained teachers with ways to more effectively accomplish those goals? A suspicious teacher committed to the social-science approach will also wonder whether there is anything about the application of computers in an educational setting that will contradict the content being presented. But this question cannot be answered with a simple yes or no. The social-science approach will evaluate each application, because for one learning objective the computer may be inappropriate, while for another it would be a very effective tool.

This book does not attempt to evaluate each potential use

of computers in light of the various approaches to religious education. That task is left to the reader. Computers are presented rather as a resource which must be evaluated by each educator, just as a new printed resource needs to be evaluated. The first step in this evaluation is to clarify overall goals and the approach that is to be taken toward religious education. The second step is to define computers and identify their capabilities.

What Do Computers Do?

Educators recognize immediately how silly it is to say, "I don't want to know anything about how computers work. Just show me how to use it." A librarian would never say, "I don't need to learn how to read. Just teach me how to check out books." Just as it is important for licensed drivers to understand that cars need gasoline, oil, and water, it is important for religious educators to have a sense of what computers need to function and how they can be used effectively.

This does not mean it is necessary for all religious educators to become expert programmers or specialists in electronic engineering. But they will need to have a general idea about the capabilities of computers, the equipment that is required, and some of the signs that problems are developing. Most of the necessary technical skills will be learned with early experience, just as drivers recognize when they have a flat tire and know that tires need to have air. Since this book assumes no previous knowledge or experience with computers, the following section briefly describes what computers do. A glossary containing words religious educators are likely to encounter is provided at the end of the book.

What can a computer do? Computers do only one thing: They manipulate electronic symbols. These symbols have no meaning for the computer—people provide the meaning for the symbols. The computer does not care whether the symbols have been defined by an English-speaking person or by a Chinese-speaking person. Any symbol can be translated into an electronic symbol. Computers are most commonly used to translate the letters of the alphabet into unique electronic symbols. When a key is pressed on a typewriter-like keyboard, the computer creates the symbol for that letter and stores it in an electronic device. Later, the computer can put the symbols on a screen or send them to a printer which will type out the letters.

Computers can also respond in different ways, depending upon the symbols. For example, at a certain point, the computer might wait for a user to press a key on the keyboard to provide it with another symbol. When that symbol is received, the computer compares it with the symbols it expects to receive. If the symbol is a Y, the computer might display the symbols that were previously entered for the children who attended church school last Sunday. The computer is only putting a pattern of dots on a screen, but the person recognizes them as the names of children.

To understand how a computer uses electronic symbols, imagine that a computer is giving a student a test. The computer translates a set of electronic symbols into dots on a television screen. The dots form the shape of letters which make up a question. The student types an answer on a keyboard. The computer translates the answer into electronic symbols and then compares this set of symbols with the symbols that have been defined as the correct answer. If the symbols are the same, the electronic symbol which indicates the number of correct responses is changed to show one more correct answer. Internally, the computer uses a set of electronic symbols to present a question, to judge whether the answer is correct, and to keep track of the number of correct answers. All uses of computers are simply expansions of this simple application, since the only thing computers can do is manipulate electronic symbols.

Notes

1. Harold William Burgess, *An Invitation to Religious Education* (Birmingham: Religious Education Press, 1975), p. 48.
2. Ibid., p. 63.
3. Ibid., p. 95.
4. *The Shape of Religious Instruction; The Flow of Religious Instruction; The Content of Religious Instruction.*
5. Burgess, *Invitation to Religious Education,* p. 132.

CHAPTER TWO

COMPUTERS IN EDUCATION

I T would be simpler to determine the appropriate way to use computers for religious education if professional educators had reached a consensus about computer use in public schools. But this has not yet been clearly defined. In 1984, Terrel Bell, the U. S. Secretary of Education and a critic of the way schools use computers, appointed a task force to discuss ways technology can improve American education. But the issues related to technology cannot be separated from the much larger issues of what education is and how it should be accomplished. As observed by one member of the task force, Carlos Benitez, president of the United Schools of America in Miami, "The general problem is that we are still using the same methods of teaching that we did 80 years ago. We still have one teacher to 30 students."[1]

It is unlikely that this government task force will provide definitive answers to questions about the proper relationship between computers and education. But under the leadership of Bell's successor, William Bennett, the task force continues to probe. Certainly, religious education will not be immune to the influences of changes in the educational approach of public schools. Some of the task force members are openly talking about radical changes. Task force chairperson William Ridley says, "We hope that the policy makers around the country will read and act upon our report. The present school system is not meeting the needs of students. We are superimposing new technology on an old system, which has got to be changed."[2]

We can be sure that the application of computer technology to education will involve dealing with the broader issues of purpose and methods. For the religious educator this is a special opportunity to bring a sensitivity of values, morals, and theology to the discussion, not only within the religious community but in society at large. At the same time religious educators are lamenting the lack of help from the secular community, there can be rejoicing that their own work can have a positive impact upon the direction of technology as used in education in general.

While religious educators cannot simply appropriate the applications and methods of computer use in secular education, there are lessons to be learned from the work that has been done. A brief review of the general use of computers in education will help set the stage for consideration of their use in religious education. There is already enough positive evidence that computers can be used effectively to justify investigating their use in religious education.

After reviewing the literature on early experiences with computers in classrooms, Johnny Lawton and Vera T. Gerschner wrote, "Research repeatedly showed that children found computers to: (a) never get tired, (b) never get frustrated or angry, (c) never forget to correct or praise, and (d) individualize learning." They cite another school where "students liked computers because they: (a) were self-paced, (b) did not embarrass students who made mistakes, (c) gave immediate feedback, and (d) left a general feeling that students learned better through the computer system." Students also felt that computers were more objective than teachers.[3]

In 1982, a report titled "Small Computers Get Big Results in Dallas Classrooms" claimed that computers work because they are impartial to ethnicity, are great motivators, are excellent for drill and practice, and are structured to teach children in small increments.[4] Computers are also noted for their ability to enhance spelling.

Early research, however, shows that computers do not

assist all children to the same degree. Hoffman and Waters found that "learning by means of a computer-assisted instructional program would seem to favor those who have the ability to quietly concentrate, are able to pay attention to details, have an affinity for memorizing facts, and can stay with a single task until completion."[5]

In a pilot project conducted by Johns Hopkins Center for Social Organization of Schools, all teachers expressed satisfaction with the "enrichment" program. But most noted the intellectual demands the computer placed on them. Overall, they felt good about the challenge and believed the project was a success. All the teachers involved also felt that a single computer in each classroom was insufficient.[6]

Present-day Use of Computers in Education

Most computer use in schools falls into six categories:

1. Drill and Practice: Using computers for student practice of skills, the principles of which are taught by the teacher in traditional ways.

2. Tutorial Dialog: Using computers to present information to students, diagnose student misunderstandings, and provide remedial instructive communication and individually designed practice.

3. Management of Instruction *(used jointly with computer-based drill and practice, or with a separate test-scoring system, or independent of either)*: Using computers to provide the teacher with automatic reporting of individual student performances and appropriate assignment of skill levels.

4. Simulation and Model-building: Using computer programs to demonstrate the consequences of a system of assumptions or the consequences of varying an assumption, usually in conjunction with instruction in science or social studies.

5. Teaching Computer-related Information Skills: Using the computer to teach students; having them apply such skills as typing, editing text, and retrieving information from computer systems.

6. Teaching Computer Programming: Having students learn to program computers to solve problems that are part of their mathematics curriculum, or simply for the understanding of programming itself.

As Henry Becker points out in his presentation of the material from the project, this list could be expanded, but most applications today will fall into one of these categories. Since each of these approaches has possible analogies in religious education, educators in that field will benefit from a closer examination of these major uses.

Drill and Practice

The first two categories, computer-based drill and practice, and tutorial dialog, are the most common uses of computers in classrooms and are often referred to as computer-assisted instruction, or C.A.I. These C.A.I. programs are based on repetitive stimulation from the computer and immediate reinforcement. In its simplest form, the computer program is little more than a workbook, with a programmed learning lesson appearing on a screen rather than on a printed page. For example, the computer might ask a question and wait for a response. After the student types the response on the keyboard, the computer checks to see whether that answer corresponds to the expected answer. If the answer is not correct, another opportunity to answer is given. After a certain number of incorrect answers the computer gives the expected (correct) answer. Then another question is asked. Depending upon the design of the program, the questions can be arranged at random, in ascending difficulty, or in some other order.

There has been renewed interest in programmed instruction, which lost favor several years ago when research failed to demonstrate any student improvement over other teaching methods. A common complaint was that students found it boring. However, sound and graphics can be added to create interest. The computer can also eliminate questions that are too easy for the student, since it is not necessary for all students to proceed through each question. Traditional programmed instruction materials direct the student to relevant remedial material when questions are answered incorrectly, but C.A.I. makes it possible for the student to receive immediate feedback. The computer can keep track of the history of incorrect responses and make a more sophisticated prescription of remedial work.

One reason drill and practice software programs have been introduced into classrooms is that these programs are relatively easy to write. A second factor is that traditional methods of drill and practice have not been popular with either students or teachers. Yet, alternative methods of teaching math facts or spelling words have not been successful in replacing drill and practice. Computer assistance has been viewed as a way to make drill and practice interesting.

Early studies indicate that students using computerized drill and practice increase achievement when compared to prior years or to control groups not exposed to C.A.I. As early as 1972, J. Vinsonhaler and R. Bass reported in *Educational Technology* that C.A.I. programs, in the majority of thirty experimental comparisons at ten sites, were more effective than traditional instruction in raising standardized test scores. Since that time, most studies have indicated that C.A.I. is an effective replacement for drill and practice. In summarizing the results of the research, Henry Becker writes,

> The limited evaluation research shows that computer-based drill programs can be effective, given enough equipment for each child to have sufficient access and given appropriate content, organization of classroom activity, and monitoring. . . . Research should be conducted to determine whether most of the more typical drill and practice materials available for the TRS-80's, Apples, and other microcomputers the schools are now buying are as educationally effective under more typical conditions of use as were the pioneer C.A.I. programs.[7]

In addition to the general questions that have been raised about the kind of learning that is possible with drill and practice, computers present a particular framework that may present philosophical educational problems. Particularly criticized have been those programs that do not provide explanations of the correct answer when it is presented. Such programs can encourage the student to be concerned with developing strategies to provide the computer with the correct answer, but not encourage understanding of the lesson being presented.

Tutorial Programs

Tutorial programs differ from drill and practice programs in one important way: They include analysis of incorrect performance. This analysis by the computer is then used in a variety of ways. In some programs there is a reorganization of the questions, based on the pattern of incorrect answers. Other programs provide detailed instructional feedback to the student, or an analysis to help the teacher. Usually tutorial programs minimize the use of repetition; material that has been mastered is not repeated.

There are three types of tutorial programs. Those that are merely advanced drill and practice programs look for the "correct" response. If it is not received, remedial instruction is presented. The student moves through the program in a predetermined pattern.

The second type uses "learner control." These programs are designed on the premise that the student is the best judge of whether remedial instruction is needed. In the 1970s the National Science Foundation funded a study which designed programs based on this concept. The student is provided with complete information about the course and an outline of the presentation of material. In the problem-solving mode, the student chooses between three levels of difficulty. Instructional assistance is also presented in three levels of difficulty. The student always controls the presentation of material and evaluations.

The third style of tutorial program adopts exactly the opposite approach. The computer is in complete control of the presentation of both remedial and new material. New material is presented when the program determines that the student is prepared to go on to the next step. This approach is sometimes called intelligent C.A.I.

Tutorial C.A.I. has advocates, but its application has been very limited, partly because of the difficulty of collecting and organizing all the information necessary to write a program that covers a substantial amount of material. If the program responds to the answers of the student, responses must be prepared for a variety of answers; programs which include material at several levels are very difficult to write.

Tutorial programs that are learner-directed have not proved to be more effective at increasing achievement than those in which the computer controls the sequence of information and the difficulty of the questions and instruction. But there may be advantages to learner-controlled programs, because students develop skills they can use in other learning situations.

Tutorials which model the student's understanding of the subject matter and provide information to the student based on this analysis have an additional problem. To respond successfully to the students' answers, the computer program must be built around a model of the way people learn and the information that is most appropriate in a learning situation. The computer is asked to be a teacher, but we know so little about what makes a good teacher that we cannot design a program to fulfill this expectation in all situations.

Every teacher knows the basic principles of education. These include the need to actively involve the student in the learning process, to use practice to reinforce skills, to give positive reinforcement, and to develop student motivation. But knowledge of these principles is not sufficient to develop a computer program which responds so that most students obtain skills as efficiently as possible.

John Seely Brown has considered this problem and has suggested four areas which need to be addressed before tutorial programs can be "intelligent":

1. A practical theory of hints. If a student has no idea how to solve a problem, what information should be given?

2. An understanding of the way hints can be given in the middle of a problem-solving session. If a student has begun to solve a problem, what is the relationship between the work already done and the hint that should be given?

3. A theory of interference. If a student has started to solve a problem but then makes a mistake, when should the computer interrupt to point out the mistake?

4. A decision about the level of analysis the computer should engage in. For example, when a student makes a mistake in solving a problem, the error may be in an intermediate step that was not directly provided to the computer. Should the computer be able to deduce the error, or respond only to the information directly provided to it?[8]

In the exteme case, one could ask whether the computer should analyze the psychological state of the student. A good teacher will present material differently to a student who appears very fatigued or distracted from the way it is presented to one who is not. Should the computer analyze the student's responses for fatigue or distraction and respond appropriately?

The jury is still out on whether it will be possible to develop tutorial programs that are more effective than other methods of education. But much of the research is directed toward providing answers to the technical difficulties of effective intelligent C.A.I.

Management of Instruction

Some schools are using computers to manage the paperwork of recording attendance, classroom enrollment, inventories of teaching supplies, and students' test scores and grades. In most cases this process uses a computer for a task that was previously accomplished with paper records.

But there are some schools in which the computer either makes the record-keeping functions more efficient or provides additional information to increase effectiveness. In one school, computerization has added a new dimension to attendance records. After the records are entered, the computer compiles all the necessary statistics for the local and state school board reports. When a student has missed more than three days, the computer places an early-morning telephone call to the student's home and plays a prerecorded message, informing the parents that the student has been absent.

For years computers have been used to score and evaluate standardized tests such as the Iowa or California achievement test. Some schools are experimenting with similar methods of computer-scored evaluation to focus on weaknesses in individual students or areas where the system is deficient.

Simulation, Model Building, and Problem Solving

Noncomputerized simulations and games became popular in the late 1960s and early 1970s because they fit well with the educational theory which emphasized active participation of students and a discovery style of learning. It was thought that simulations provided situations in which students could gain experience without taking on the risks of real-life situations.

In a bold experiment, Harvard Business School built a large part of its graduate degree training program around computer simulation games. In the low-risk environment of these computer-coordinated games, students test their skill and intuition as they make business decisions. The computer presents the students with a business situation. The students decide how to use the resources that are available and give the computer information about their decisions. The computer analyzes the implications of these decisions and returns a new set of business conditions for the students to evaluate.

Simulations differ from role-playing in that the students must respond according to the rules of the game. In role-playing educational activity, there are no rules to govern possible responses. It is difficult to design these programs, since for the simulation to be of educational value, it must reflect the real world with all its constraints. But we usually do not know enough about the real world to accurately define all the rules. In cases where the simulation is easy to program, the results are so trivial that the simulation loses its educational benefit.

In addition to the formidable practical problems of preparing high quality educational simulations, research on the effectiveness of computer simulation games has failed to prove that simulations are superior to other teaching methods. Although most studies have found little or no learning advantages, they have shown that there is improvement in the attitudes of students. Some teachers will choose these games even though the only additional benefit is the students' increased interest. But early experiments with computers provided students with an opportunity to use sophisticated equipment in situations where the teachers themselves showed a great deal of interest in what was happening, so the same benefits may not be possible if computers become common in schools.

In model building, the student is involved in the process of defining the rules to govern a particular situation. Model building can be thought of as asking the student to design a simulation game. While this approach has appealed to some philosophers of education, it has proved very difficult to implement. If it is difficult to design a simulation game, it is even more difficult to design a program that will allow students to invent their own simulations. There is little information about the relative effectiveness of model-building educational techniques.

Computer-related Information Skills

Computer use in the society has placed demands on educational institutions to train students in such skills as word processing, data entry, data retrieval, and the area known as computer literacy. Educational programs which parallel those that teach children how to use a library have been devised. Students are taught how to use the computer as a tool. Just as driver education has become an integral part of a school's program, courses which provide students with the practical skills of using a computer are increasingly becoming part of the curriculum.

At the high school level, many of the computers first purchased were used to teach computer programming. In many cases this was a way to offer enrichment opportunities to students with special skills in mathematics. But a philosophical debate has raged over whether there are general educational benefits in the teaching of computer programming. On the one side it is argued that learning to program a computer teaches about learning and reality. Seymour Papert says, "Through these experiences those children would be serving their apprenticeship as epistemologists, that is to say, learning to think articulately about thinking."[9] So far, there has been little evidence that these skills are transferable to other learning situations, but the advocates of teaching computer programming to all students argue primarily from a philosophical position.

Arthur Luehrmann argues that computer programming is a skill like reading and writing.[10] Teachers could preserve the skill for themselves, but Luehrmann believes that it is far better for the teachers to teach the students reading and writing. In the same way, he says, students should be taught computer programming.

Others argue that computer programming is too complicated to teach to all students—it involves developing skills of problem formulation and solving. Educational programs such as the LOGO computer language have attempted to address the problem of the languages being too complicated for the average student to master. But there are still questions about the necessity, or even the advantage of teaching all students programming skills.

Problems with Computers in Education

Recognizing some of the problems encountered in secular education may help religious educators plan for computer use. A major problem with using computers for drill and practice or tutorial programs is that these programs are very individualized; one student uses the computer. Since schools usually purchase very few computers—sometimes only one to a classroom or three or four for the whole building—it is difficult for teachers to use them effectively.

This problem of limited availability may not last long. As computers become less expensive, it will be possible to purchase larger quantities. According to Talmis Research of New York, 630,000 computers were installed in the nation's schools at the beginning of the 1984-1985 school year.[11] By the end of that year there were more than one million. This rapid growth will increase the availability of computers to individual students.

Software availability and quality also has been a problem. Even when software is developed, it is not always identified by schoolteachers and administrators. The skills necessary to successfully evaluate and compare software are being acquired slowly. Since all software is not of equal value, the ability to choose appropriate software is very important.

The training of teachers to take full advantage of computers has presented additional problems. In most pilot projects teachers reported that there were challenges involved in using computers in situations in which other methods were more familiar. This was true even when teachers had very positive feelings about their experience with computers. Introducing computers into an educational situation results in certain changes, and changes meet with resistance, for a variety of reasons.[12]

Even the use of computers for school administration has included some drawbacks. When computers are used to record students' grades, the categories must be very clearly defined. This presented a problem at the Morrison School in Philadelphia. Computerization of the grading system forced teachers to limit their comments on the report cards. Although there is still a small amount of space for individualized comments, the computerized reporting system has many more categories, and the teachers are now asked to assign satisfactory or unsatisfactory marks to a series of questions. Previously, an individualized comment would have conveyed the progress of the student. Some teachers feel this computer-assisted administration reduces the value of the report process and sometimes results in parental confusion.

The Future of Computers in Education

Educators recognize some of the early difficulties and false starts and now look toward the future. A number of future possibilities have been suggested.

At one extreme is the possible development of a computerized "videopal." At first this sounds like something out of science fiction, but a great deal of research is being conducted, aimed at solving the problems that still exist in bringing a videopal into existence.

Imagine a student who arrives at school in the morning and checks into the terminal to say good morning to the "Pal." The Pal would ask a few questions to learn how the student is feeling. The Pal has recorded the student's previous performance and activities, so the student and the Pal would design the day's learning activities together. These might include some practice of math or language skills. The Pal would help the student choose books to read that are appropriate to the student's reading level and interests. Because the Pal communicates with the Pals of other students in the school, group projects would also be suggested when two or more students would benefit from shared activities.

Much of the student's time would be spent with the Pal in a tutorial mode. For example, a student interested in music might experiment with making melodies and adding accompaniment. The Pal would play back the creations and offer hints to help the student discover alternative ways to write and modify the tunes. While the student plays with creating music, the Pal would continually evaluate the student's activity so that it can monitor the student's development. If the student's discovery of music theory through the process of play misses some aspect that would be helpful, the Pal would either present the concept or make suggestions to help the student discover the theory.

Using this same style, the Pal would help the student discover how to solve a mathematical problem or write creatively. The Pal would encourage the student by giving positive reinforcement as skills develop and by offering hints and additional information at a level the student can understand.

But the Pal would also provide parents and professional educators with periodic evaluations. In this scenario the professional educator is completely relieved of the responsibility of presenting materials, communicating academic skills, and evaluating. All this is done by the computer, which can give individualized attention and draw on far more extensive resources than could an individual teacher. The professional educator concentrates on helping the student interpret the evaluations generated by Pal, on coordinating group activities first suggested by the Pals, and on helping the students develop interpersonal and relationship skills.

At the other extreme, some educators see the future of computers in the classroom in a much more limited role. The computer will become an assistant to the teacher, similar to a classroom aide. When the teacher discovers that a particular student needs remedial work in a certain area, the student would be assigned a computer exercise to catch up with the rest of the class. Students who progress through a topic and master it would be given enrichment by learning through a computer game or by further developing a skill through a computer exercise.

Large computer screens could be used for presentations to classes. Such a screen could be used in a physics class, for instance, to illustrate the movement of objects according to Newton's laws, and students could discuss how the objects would move with a different set of laws.

At times, students could take examinations by answering questions at computer consoles, but the computer would only score the examination; it would not perform complicated analysis.

How much further technology will develop, and whether educators will decide to use computers to radically change secular education, remains to be seen. It may be that computers will be adapted to certain tasks and will assist the educational process, but will not have any more impact on the style of education than overhead projectors or video recorders have had.

Before we become too excited about the possible changes, it is well to remember that prophets of the role of video recorders suggested that college lecturers could be replaced by video recordings of the very best teachers. They expected that college campuses would be turned into video libraries, but by the mid-1980s there is little evidence that the style of higher education has been very much affected by video recorders.

Notes

1. *Infoworld* (February 25, 1985):22.
2. Ibid.
3. Johnny Lawton and Vera T. Gerschner, "A Review of the Literature on Attitudes toward Computers and Computerized Instruction," *Journal of Research and Development in Education* 16/1(Fall 1982):51.
4. "Small Computers Get Big Results in Dallas Classrooms," *Computer 82* 3(October 1981):54-55.
5. Cited by Lawton and Gerschner: J. L. Hoffman and K. Waters, "Some Effects of Student Personality on Success with Computer-assisted Instruction," *Educational Technology* (March 1982):20-21.
6. Henry Jay Becker, *Microcomputers in the Classroom: Dreams and Realities* (Baltimore: Center for Social Organization of Schools, Johns Hopkins University, 1982), p.15. The next section follows the Johns Hopkins report.
7. Ibid., pp. 20-21.
8. John Seely Brown, "Uses of Artificial Intelligence and Advanced Computer Technology in Education," in *Computers and Communication*, Robert J. Seidel and Martin Rubin, eds. (New York: Academic Press, 1977).
9. Seymour Papert, *Mindstorms* (New York: Basic Books, 1980), p. 27.
10. Arthur Luehrmann, *Should the Computer Teach the Student, or Vice Versa?"* (Washington, D.C.: Association for Information Processing Systems, 1972).
11. *Infoworld*
12. Becker, *Microcomputers in the Classroom*, p. 13.

CHAPTER THREE

LET'S BE PRACTICAL

WILL computers that can be used for the educational ministry of the church soon be less expensive? If we buy them now, will they be obsolete in a few years? Will the software that is likely to be produced by the education division of the denomination for use in the churches require specific computers? All three questions must be answered, "Yes, probably." So the practical person will ask: Should we purchase computers for religious education now, and if so, which ones?

For a moment, let's put aside all questions about whether computers can be used effectively in religious education. Assuming that they do have a place, what are some of the practical considerations?

Shop for Software First

The most common answer to the question, What computer should we buy? is: Don't shop for a computer—choose your software first. Usually this is a very good idea, but in religious education, there are several problems. First, because there are so many possible uses for the computer in religious education, a church must choose one that will provide the greatest benefit to the most people. Second, the development of religious education software is in its infancy; there will certainly be much more available in the future.

The first problem is not trivial. Let's imagine a situation in which, after due consideration, it is decided that the best software for the minister to use with the confirmation class is a program written for an Apple II computer. The preschool that meets at the church has discovered some excellent software designed to help children understand and remember the order of events in Bible stories. This program is written for a Commodore 64. The church school treasurer saw the treasurer at a neighboring church using an Osborne computer to keep the church school books. And the junior high leader has been very impressed with programs for the DEC Rainbow, designed to encourage class interaction and faith development.

In such a situation, it is very difficult to be practical. But it is possible to begin to deal with the problem. In 1985, Digital Electronics Corporation stopped manufacturing the DEC Rainbow, and the future of the machine is in question. Although there may be excellent software already written, it is very unlikely that more will be developed for this machine. Discontinued computers are not a wise choice, because additional software probably will not be available in the future.

The Osborne computer, which the treasurer liked, uses what is called a CP/M operating system. This means that it can use the software of many other computers. Any computer with the CP/M operating system can use the same software. At first this sounds very good, but neither the Commodore 64 nor the Apple has the CP/M operating system. (It is necessary to have a special hardware adapter to use CP/M software with either of these computers.) Since it is likely that software for the church school treasurer can be found for either the Apple or the Commodore 64, administrative uses of the computer can be studied after the classroom software has been chosen. It is probable that adequate administrative software will be available for use with any computer.

But this church still has the problem of choosing between an Apple and a Commodore 64. Each of these has its own operating system, so software cannot be exchanged between them. Some attempts have been made to design plug-in boards or cartridges to make a computer accept software written for another machine, but these add-on products do not always work with educational software. The best educational software is designed to take full advantage of the capabilities of a given computer. This is particularly true of software that uses graphics capabilities. The sad fact is that in the mid-1980s, there is no computer for sale that will flawlessly run all educational software regardless of the computer it was written for. So it is necessary to compromise.

Deciding which computer or computers to purchase is actually little different from deciding on a copying machine. Religious educators must think about the needs they have, match these with the equipment that is available, and make sure they are buying at a fair price.

But there is another variable—possible future software development. Denominations may develop software for a specific computer. This potential problem is complicated by the possibility that the computer a denomination settles on may not even be invented yet. It is impossible to know what the future will hold, but it is still best to obtain computers that are most likely to be able to use the software of the future.

Guessing the Future

The wisest move is to choose a computer manufactured by a company that is likely to stay in business and produce high quality equipment. Applying this wisdom in 1983, one probably would have purchased a TI 99/4, manufactured by the Texas Instrument Company. That computer was very inexpensive, but it had excellent color graphics and sound capabilities, making it an obvious choice for people interested in developing educational software. It was made by a multinational corporation, a leader in the manufacture of computer component parts. Although the Texas Instrument Company is still in business and still manufactures computers, the TI 99/4 is no longer being made. It is almost certain that no religious education software for that machine will be developed in the future.

There is no way to avoid the ambiguities or uncertainties of the future. But this is no reason to delay. A church can obtain computer equipment that can be put to immediate use with the software currently available and that also has the potential of being of use in the future as more software is developed.

How Many Computers Does a Church School Need?

Although we cannot know what software will be available in the future, it is possible to decide the style to be used in a particular religious education situation. The first style is that of limiting the use of a computer to management of the religious education program. This would require only a single computer, which might also be used for other administrative tasks in the church. Computers that are likely candidates for use only in administration are discussed at the end of this section.

At the other extreme is the style of attempting to use computers as the core of an instructional program. Each student would need to have a computer available; there would be either a personal computer for each student or a group of computer terminals linked to a central station, where a teacher would monitor each terminal. The church school classroom would look like a computer laboratory.

Between these two extremes are a variety of other styles. A single computer can be used as one activity center in a room containing many activity centers. Alternatively, it could be used with a large screen, to be viewed by a group of children.

Public schools have learned that it is impossible to effectively use software designed for one student, who will spend six hours a week at the computer terminal, with a group of 100 students and one computer. The problem is even more exaggerated in the church school, with students present only one hour a week. If computer time were equally divided in a church school class of twenty members,

41

one computer would make it possible for each student to spend just over two and a half hours per year at the computer. It seems likely that trying to schedule computer time in such a class would cause so much disruption that any educational benefits would be completely negated.

From a practical point of view, a church would either need to have a large number of computers available; adopt a style of religious education that uses activity centers, so that a single computer is not disruptive; or use the computer only in group activities. The point is that it is important to purchase equipment that makes it possible to use the software that is purchased: Software designed for a single user demands a computer for each user; software designed for group activities cannot be used effectively in a room filled with equipment.

Setting up a Computer Laboratory

First, let us look at the possibilities of setting up a small computer lab in the church school classroom, where each student would have a computer available for individualized instruction.

It is impossible to calculate a cost-effective ratio for computers in religious education. Because computers cost the same, whether they are used one hour a week on Sunday morning or several hours every day, it is just good stewardship to consider ways a computer lab can be used in conjunction with a day school or with an after-school program.

The cost can be reduced by using a network of computers which share some equipment, such as disk drives and printers. For example, PETSCAN makes it possible for up to 37 Commodore PET computers to be connected to a single system. One problem is that this system is designed for use with the older Commodore PET computer rather than the more popular and less expensive Commodore 64. Tandy Corporation sells a network controller through its Radio Shack Computer centers. This system allows up to 16 TRS-80 computers to be connected to a host computer. The controller makes it possible for a classroom of students to use software programs that are distributed to each computer station by the teacher. With this network, the students cannot control the disk drive or printer.

A computer lab with ten individual work stations using the PETSCAN system costs between $7,000 and $8,000. Software is an additional expense. The Radio Shack system, using TRS-80 Color Computers, costs about half as much.

Using Individualized Computers

Because computers are becoming less expensive each year, there will be churches where setting up a learning center with ten or fifteen computer stations makes sense. In the mid-1980s the three most likely candidates for church computer labs are the Commodore 64, the Radio Shack Color Computer, and the Atari 800XL.

The discussion that follows should not be used to make a decision about which computer to purchase. Manufacturers may change specifications, and computers with new designs will certainly become available. These examples are merely to illustrate the characteristics of computer equipment and show how comparisons can be made.

The Atari 800XL has the best graphics capabilities of any of the computers discussed here; software designers can use 256 different colors. The Commodore 64 uses 16 different colors; the Radio Shack Color Computer, only eight. With the Atari 800XL, there are 11 different ways to set up graphics, using various levels of resolution and foreground and background configurations. The Color Computer has three graphics modes; the Commodore 64, only two. In addition, the Atari 800XL has five text modes and also produces music, using a four-voice sound generator. The Commodore 64 comes very close in its ability to play music—it uses a three-voice generator; but the Radio Shack Color Computer has limited ability in this area.

Although the Atari 800XL would be an excellent computer for religious education software that uses sound and graphics, software developers have not used this computer to its full advantage. Arcade-type games are its strong suit. Although there is little religious education software written for any computer, a church planning to use software written by others should be aware that the Commodore 64 has much more than the Atari. It also has more programs for other applications.

Since the Commodore 64 is the most successful computer sold to date, there has been much serious software development for this machine. This computer is also supported by a wide variety of peripheral devices— modems, printers, light pens, graphic pads, and plotters. Most users will find the Commodore 64 as versatile as the Atari 800XL, since the Atari's full capacity for music and graphics is seldom used. The larger software library available is a real plus for the Commodore.

The Radio Shack Color Computer cannot compete with either the Atari 800XL or the Commodore 64, on a point for point comparison of characteristics, but the Color Computer has the advantage of excellent manufacturer support. Service and training are available at all Radio Shack Computer centers. For most uses, the excellent graphics of the Radio Shack Color Computer are more than adequate, and if a church is going to develop its own software, the BASIC programming software that comes with the Color Computer is a plus. Although BASIC is a very powerful language, it is excellent for beginning programmers, and this computer, because of its more limited graphic and sound capabilities, is less intimidating.

Radio Shack also sells an optional operating system, OS-9, a version of the Unix operating system. With this system it is possible to gain experience with the multitasking and multiuser functions of computers.

The Atari 800XL, the Commodore 64, and the Radio Shack Color Computer can all be connected to television sets; they have similar screen resolution. The Commodore 64 and the Atari 800XL can be connected to computer monitors, and it is possible to purchase a version of the Radio Shack Color Computer that can be connected to a computer monitor. But the computers being considered here will benefit only slightly from a computer monitor. (In technical language, they display 250 to 320 pixels horizontally and 190 to 200 vertically.) One of the implications of this video resolution is that the computers display large letters when used for word processing. With the Radio Shack Color Computer, only 32 letters are displayed on each line. Both the Commodore 64 and the Atari 800XL display 40 characters per line.

If a computer will be used for group activities rather than as a single work station for one student, then the monitor would be a major consideration. Obviously it would be impossible to use a computer with a six-inch screen for a group of 15 children. Although a television screen does not provide the high resolution possible with some computer monitors, projection screens are large enough so that a group of people can see the computer output. With large screens, the Atari 800XL, the Commodore 64, and the Radio Shack Color Computer can all be used for group activities.

It is always necessary to have an off-line storage device for information and software when the computer is turned off. With the three computers discussed here, there are two possibilities: a cassette tape recorder or a floppy disk drive. Without off-line storage, it would be necessary to type software into the computer each time it is to be used. Some software, such as arcade games, is available in cartridges which plug into the computer. It is unlikely, however, that very much religious education software will be distributed in cartridges.

The advantage of a cassette tape system is that it is inexpensive. Any tape recorder can be used with the Radio Shack Color Computer. An adapter is necessary for both the Commodore 64 and the Atari 800XL unless a cassette recorder designed specifically for the computer is used. There are several problems, however, associated with using a cassette recorder for off-line storage. The first is reliability: It is important to make several copies of software and data, because sometimes the recorder has difficulty retrieving information. The second problem is expedition:

Cassette recorders are very slow. A long or complicated program may take as much as twenty minutes to load into the computer. When large amounts of information will be used by the computer, a cassette system does not work. But if the computer will be used in an educational setting in which software is only loaded into the computer and the computer is then used by a student without saving any data, it is acceptable to spend three or four minutes at the beginning of a session loading the software from a cassette player.

For educational applications, a single disk drive is usually sufficient. With a single disk drive, the computer reads information from one floppy disk at a time. If that disk does not contain all the necessary information for a particular application, it is removed and a second disk is placed in the drive. With a floppy disk, software can be loaded into a computer in a matter of seconds.

Other Computers to Consider

Some computers are distinguished by a certain operating system such as CP/M or MS-DOS (the system used by IBM-compatible computers). Others can be grouped by their central processing unit—the chip—the component where the actual computing takes place. For example, IBM-PC computers use an 8088 chip. The Amiga from Commodore, the 520ST from Atari, and the Macintosh from Apple all use a 68000 chip, the most powerful chip used by any of the computers discussed in this book. Computers using this chip are of particular interest to educators because they are well suited to graphics and sound production.

The Macintosh was the first mass-marketed computer to use the 68000 chip. This computer was not designed as an educational tool, but was intended to be a business computer like the IBM-PC. Expense alone might eliminate it from consideration in an educational setting. But the machine demonstrates some of the features that will be common in computers of the near future. For instance, small pictures called *icons* will identify the options for a user. With the Macintosh, the user slides a small box, a *mouse*, on the table to move an arrow on the screen. When the arrow points at a particular icon and a button on the mouse is pressed, the computer will accomplish a certain function. Complicated programs can be used by people who do not have highly developed typing skills.

The sophisticated graphics capability of the Macintosh makes it possible to produce interesting screen displays or printed materials with a variety of type styles. Although there has been very little educational software developed for the Macintosh, the machine illustrates new possibilities for educational use of computers. For example, several programs can be displayed on the screen at once, each in an area called a window. It would be possible to have an educational adventure game which demands a knowledge of the book of Acts in one window; the student could move to another window to call up a particular verse; and notes for future reference could be made in a third window.

Both the Amiga and the 520ST were introduced late in 1985. They have color display, while the Macintosh has only black and white. The Amiga comes with an operating system capable of multitasking—it can use several programs at the same time. In the future a student may be able to work with one program while another program evaluates his or her responses so that appropriate educational activities can be suggested. Educators will also be interested in the Amiga's sophisticated audio capabilities. Spoken words as well as sounds and music can be part of computerized education, since the Amiga is delivered with text-to-speech software that can make the computer "talk."

The 520ST is the least expensive of the 68000 computers and therefore is a likely candidate for early development of religious education software. As well as a sophisticated graphics system and an easy-to-use approach, the 520ST has several additional features of interest to educators. There is an adapter for attaching a musical instrument digital interface (MIDI). It also has the ability to be used with a CD ROM, sometimes called an optical-disk drive.

This device uses disks similar to those used in audio compact disk players. A single disk can store the equivalent of five encyclopedias of information. Four or five disks will hold more information than can be found in most church libraries. These CD ROMs offer exciting possibilities for religious educators. In the very near future, they will provide an inexpensive way for resouce materials to be published and distributed.

In addition to those we have been discussing, there are a number of other computers that should be considered for use in religious education: Apple II computers, IBM and IBM compatible computers, and computers that use the CP/M operating system.

Today Apple II computers are available in several forms. Apple IIe and Apple II Plus have expansion slots so that computer hardware may be added to enhance their operation. The Apple IIc is the most recent version. It uses most of the software written for previous versions, but is designed to be an inexpensive computer for the person who is not a hobbyist.

Because Apple II computers included graphic capabilities, they were the choice of many early designers of educational software, so that today there is a large quantity available, including software specifically for religious education. Because of the popularity of these computers, there are many people who are experienced Apple II programmers. Although the original computer was designed in the mid-1970s, new versions have taken advantage of advances in technology, so that it is competitive with more recent brands. Because the new versions have preserved software compatibility with the older Apple II computers, the software base has continued to grow, and it is likely that more religious education software will be developed in the future.

When IBM introduced a personal computer, it was an instant hit. Not only did the business community like the idea of buying a personal computer from IBM, but some schools set up laboratories with these computers. The software industry dedicated itself to creating a large collection of software, including much for educational application.

Although an IBM PC or one of the computers designed to use IBM PC software can be used for education, it seems unlikely that the IBM PC will become the computer of choice for educational use in the future, partly because IBM computers have been more expensive than the others we have mentioned. When ten or twenty are purchased, the cost difference can be substantial. These computers have found their greatest use in business settings, and an IBM PC could very well be used in the administration of a religious education program.

Computers with CP/M operating systems include Kaypro II and 4, Osborne computers, Televideo, and numerous others. An operating system is a set of instructions which make the computer function properly. Because these computers share a common operating system, software written for one machine will work on the others. These computers have seen their greatest use in business, since excellent software for administration has been written for them. But very little educational software exists for these computers, and it is unlikely that there will be an effort to prepare more in the future. However, because they are often less expensive than IBM PC and computers that use IBM PC software, they could be considered for religious education administration.

Computers with CP/M operating systems are not particularly well suited to educational use because this system does not have good graphic capabilities. Although there is a common operating system, it does not include a common system for printing information on the computer screen. Therefore programs that use graphics are still specific to a particular brand of computer and cannot be moved from one machine to another.

There are other computers to choose from. After the characteristics of individual computers are compared, the final choice must consider very seriously the availability of software (the ease with which software can be written or purchased) and the probability that future software developments will make a particular computer a wise choice.

Can the Purchase of Computers Be Justified?

There is one question that persists: Can a church school, which meets only one hour a week, ever justify investment in computers? Even the least expensive system with a screen large enough for a group of children to view will cost close to $1,000. A small ten-computer learning center where students can interact individually with the computer will cost at least $5,000 or $6,000. Software will be an additional expense. Given the fact that the cost of computers continues to fall, one might ask, How inexpensive will computers need to become before their cost can be justified?

Justifying investment in computers for religious education rests on the demonstration of their effectiveness in helping a church school accomplish its goals. The teachers and administrators involved in the program are a major contributing factor. Equipment and teaching aids that are used very effectively by one teacher may not work at all with another. This is true, whether the aid be flannel boards, overhead projectors, or computers. The volunteer teachers in church schools will be critical in determining whether computers, at any cost, are effective.

During the early stages of computer use in religious education, the situations most likely to justify the cost of computer equipment are those in which there is a high level of motivation on the part of the church school staff to make computers work.

Other Alternatives

There are several alternatives to having computer equipment that is used only on Sunday morning and sits idle at all other times. For example, some retail computer stores have laboratories where they conduct training sessions with the computers they sell. These facilities are seldom used on Sunday morning. Arrangements might be made for a church school class to meet at a computer store and use the computers there. This approach could greatly reduce the cost; the major expense would be software.

Another approach involves looking for ways the computer equipment could be put to use at other times. Churches with preschool nursery programs or parochial schools could use the computers for programs beyond religious education. Even churches without weekday education programs might make their computers available for additional educational use. There may be ways the computers could be used in mission to the community.

Computers used in another setting could be moved to the church school on Sunday, but it would be a large task to disconnect them and set them up in a new place, only to repeat the process several hours later.

Most of the portable or transportable computers are not well suited to educational use. Transportable computers weigh about twenty or thirty pounds. Kaypro and Compaq computers are transportables. These have a built-in monitor screen too small to be used with a group of people, but some transportables can be connected to larger monitors so that they could be used with a group.

The smaller machines called lap computers may have sufficient computing power to be used for education, but they usually have a very small display. Computers like the Radio Shack Model 100 or Model 200 weigh less than five pounds and can operate on batteries, but because the equipment is not well suited to an educational setting, there is little educational software available for them.

A computer used in the church office for administration might be used effectively for religious education. It is likely to be either an IBM PC or compatible computer, or one of those with a CP/M operating system. As mentioned above, these may not be the first choice for educational use, but they might be used in limited ways with church school classes. In the near future, church offices will be installing multiuser systems, so that more than one work station can be connected to a central computer. When this becomes common, church schools may decide to use inexpensive terminals connected to this central system.

Some of the early experiments in religious education were with terminals connected by telephone lines to a large distant computer. While this is still one possible way to obtain computer accessibility, it is seldom cost-effective. If the central computer is not nearby, there will be telephone toll charges. Even when the terminals in the church are connected to a local computer, the cost of terminals is very near the cost of complete computers adequate for most religious education uses today. One advantage of using a terminal connected to a distant computer is that many users share it, so that it is possible to have the computing power of a very powerful and expensive computer without paying the full cost. But for most religious education applications, even the least expensive computer is powerful enough.

As another strategy, a church might take advantage of the home computers of its members. A survey of the congregation may turn up enough home computers to be used by the church. Some of the early experiments involved having children work on a computer program at home, with the support and help of parents.

Used and Discontinued Computers

As computers become more common, used computers are becoming available. The best ones would be the fairly new models that are still being manufactured, since it is possible to find support for them and it is more likely that software will continue to be available. Sometimes these are available because the owner is moving up to a larger computer.

Used computers of a model no longer being made but manufactured by a company that is still in the computer business are a second choice. Examples are the Apple III and Radio Shack Model I. Although new software is unlikely to be developed for these machines, the hardware will be supported.

There are several things to watch for when shopping for a

used computer. Make sure the screen produces a sharp, clear image without a flicker. Look for burn spots on the tube or "blooms" when it is turned on. Although a screen can be replaced, a bad screen is an indication that the computer has been given very hard use or has been neglected.

Check to see that none of the keys on the keyboard stick and that all the connecting ports operate correctly. It is also a good idea to check the disk drive by testing it with one of the original disks supplied with software. The disk drive may need alignment. Sometimes older disk drives will work perfectly well with disks that have been formatted on the disk drive, but will not read disks supplied by a software manufacturer.

Money may also be saved on equipment by purchasing new discontinued models. Although discontinued models are often sold at discount prices, the problems are similar to those encountered when purchasing used equipment.

Conclusion

Investment in computer equipment should not be casual. Careful attention should be given to planning how it will be used and the way it will affect the educational ministry of the church. Consideration of these issues will ultimately determine what computer equipment may be needed and whether it is practical to obtain it.

Even more important than the consideration of hardware and software is the interest of the teachers and staff. If the people who will be using computer-assisted instruction are highly motivated to use computers, as well as to be effective religious educators, there is a much greater probability that the computers will be used effectively.

The most practical approach is to talk with the people who will be using the computers, devise a clear plan for computer assistance with the educational program, determine what software will be needed, and then find equipment that can be used.

CHAPTER FOUR

COMPUTERS
IN THE
CLASSROOM

THE use of computers in church school classrooms will parallel their use in public school classrooms, reviewed in a previous chapter. Three types of use are considered here: a computer laboratory setting, where each student interacts individually with a computer; group activities with a computer; and computer preparation of materials for use in the church school classroom.

Software Evaluation

Whether computers are used by individuals or as the center of a group activity, it is important to carefully evaluate software for quality and appropriateness. In many ways the choice of software is based on a subjective evaluation. What one teacher or group of students finds useful may not work at all in another setting. But it is possible to define some of the characteristics of high quality educational software. Former Secretary of Education T. H. Bell expressed concern about the quality of software:

> We need at the earliest possible time to develop much more effective software that utilizes the full potential of the computer's artificial intelligence to interact with the minds of learners. Too much computer software is simply electronic page turning, and it has little advantage over a well-illustrated book. What we need is a major effort to develop some super software packages that will:

1. Motivate the students through reaching into the interests and concerns of the minds of the learners;

2. Branch out and present the subject matter again and again to the learner who did not grasp the concept the first time it was presented;

3. Move ahead rapidly with the gifted and talented learners;

4. Present the subject matter with the utmost in attractive sound, color, and animation;

5. Reinforce the students' desire to learn more by offering prompts, cues, and encouragement in working through some of the most crucial phases of some lessons; and

6. Keep careful tabulation of each student's progress, correct any erroneous responses, and print the same out for use of the teacher. . . .

We have a long way to go to reach a level where our computer software meets the criteria I cited above. But the potential is so promising that we ought to be aggressively pushing an educational software development effort on a much more massive scale.[1]

Religious educators who decide to use only software that will measure up to these high standards will find very little for a church school classroom. This does not mean that it is impossible to find software that will be beneficial.

The National Education Association Educational Computer Service has developed a process to evaluate educational software. The complete process is described in a document called *Guide to the Software Assessment Procedure Reviewer Document #1: Courseware,* available from NEA Educational Computer Service. A complete checklist is used to evaluate software.

Since this evaluation process, designed to occur in a classroom with the regular teacher, is completely independent of the content of the material presented in the software, a similar process could be used to evaluate religious software. A denomination or group of churches could adopt a similar procedure, but the process involves using the software in a classroom situation. And a church school teacher needs to be able to make a judgment about software before it is used in the classroom. Below is a list of things to consider when looking at a particular software product.[2]

1. **Does it work?** Make sure it actually does what it claims to do. The fact that a software product is being sold does not necessarily mean it will function properly. Sometimes it is poorly written or designed, or it may have been written for specific equipment and is not suited to yours. For example, software written to be used with a color monitor may not work with a black and white television. Do not try to use software that does not function properly. The distraction caused by problems with the software (or hardware) will negate any positive benefits of using the computer.

2. **Is the program educationally accurate?** If the content of the material presented is inconsistent with the beliefs taught, the program should not be used. Religious education software will vary in its theological approach, just as other religious education materials vary. Educational programs designed by and used in one church may not be appropriate in another. A church school teacher can immediately identify software that is inconsistent in tone or content with the theology and philosophy of education of the church school.

3. **Is the program interesting?** Using a computer may engage the interest of some students, regardless of the content of the software. But intrigue with the machine will last a very short time. Software varies greatly in its ability to hold the attention of students. Sound and graphic presentation is one way to provide stimulation and interest, but this is not essential. Software that presents pages to be read from the screen will probably not hold the interest of students. At the outset, church school teachers will have difficulty discovering the kinds of presentations students find interesting, but over time a sense of what works will develop, just as it does with other teaching methods.

4. Is the material appropriate for the age level of the class? A software program that works well with preschool children will seem very childish to twelve-year-olds. Check the sophistication of the material presented, the style of presentation, and the level of sophistication needed to operate the programs. If a program is designed for third-graders, it is important that the instructions or responses are not written at an eighth-grade reading level. Putting pictures in their proper order may interest first-graders but seem silly to tenth-graders.

5. Is the program easy to use? The purpose of using the computer is to teach religious education, not to develop sophisticated computer users. Instructions for using the program should be logical and in nontechnical language. The best programs will include help functions, enabling a student to ask for help in making the program function properly. Instructions should always be present on the screen, so that the student can concentrate on the material rather than on how to make the computer work. If a program is difficult to use, it would be better to find another method of presenting the material.

Sometimes programs need to be tried before one knows whether they are useful. But certain programs can be eliminated immediately by asking the five questions above. Each teacher also will have criteria that is specific to that teacher or to the situation. For example, a church's available computer equipment will make it impossible to use some software. And some teachers may want to use only software that is clearly Bible-centered, just as they use only printed material that is centered on the Scriptures.

Even if software meets the minimum requirements listed above, there still may be a need to decide between different software products. Some programs will be better than others. Marydel Frohne published the principles she uses when developing software or evaluating software developed by others:

*Is the program "user friendly"? Any person with no prior computer experience should be able to follow directions throughout the program.

*Does it give the learner "feedback" and positive reinforcement? The learner needs to see that his responses are correct or understand why they are incorrect. Self-scoring devices should be used whenever possible.

*Does it stimulate "higher level" intellectual skills? Questions should call for responses that require rule-application or creative thinking. A program that is too simple will not motivate learners or help them grow.

*Does it maintain interest? At present the hardware itself is highly motivational—it's a novelty. But with increased use of video-arcade type games, young people tire quickly of more serious programs based on textual material. Most programs now available are dull, due to lack of color and sound. But we must seek to find motivational factors within the content and what it teaches about the faith, more than in the software packaging of that content.

*Does it stimulate creativity?[3]

Because computers will be only one part of the religious education activities of a church, software needs to be evaluated in relation to the total educational program. There is no reason to be intimidated by the prospect of evaluating software. The religious education work of the church is presently being evaluated; the same process can be used with computer software. There is really only one question: Will the use of particular software make religious education more enjoyable and effective?

Computer Lab

A computer laboratory is a room which contains sufficient computers so that each child can use an individual set of equipment. In this setting it is possible to have all the children learning the same material, or each child can choose or be assigned different material. Most educational software is designed for a laboratory setting.

Home Computer Software of Canoga Park, California, has developed a program called "Ten Questions." Students who have played the game Twenty Questions will quickly pick up the rules. The computer chooses a person, place, or thing related to the Bible and presents clues one at a time. After each clue the student is asked to guess what the computer is "thinking of." The computer responds with music or a beep to incorrect answers and gives another clue. If the student cannot make a guess, pressing the return button advances to the next clue. If the answer the computer is looking for is not entered before ten clues have been given, the answer is provided by the computer. The content of this software program is controlled by the designers. All characters, places, and objects have been written into the program.

The same software authors also have written a program in which the student controls the content. "Teach Me Characters" is exactly the opposite of "Ten Questions." When using this software, the student thinks of a Bible character and the computer tries to guess the right answer. At first it is very easy to trick the computer because the original program includes very few characters. The computer asks a question about the character, such as "Is this character in the Old Testament?" The student answers yes or no. If the student, having chosen Paul as the character, answers no, the computer asks a question which distinguishes between characters in the New Testament. For example, the computer asks, "Is the character a disciple?" If the student answers no, the computer guesses, "Is the character Titus?" This time the student has tricked the computer, so the computer asks, "What question will distinguish between Titus and Paul?" The student might type in, "Did the character write a letter to the church in Rome?" Then the computer asks whether yes or no is the answer for Paul. Now the program has been taught steps that will lead it to Paul. The answers are permanently stored on a disk, so that the next time the program is used, the computer will know how to guess Paul.

This program can be used to help a student develop skill in distinguishing between biblical characters. It is also possible to use the program as a quiz. For example, the students could be assigned the task of teaching the computer to guess the names of all twelve disciples. After each student has entered questions which allow the computer to distinguish between the disciples, the students could exchange disks.

A company called C-4 Resources, of Champaign, Illinois, has designed educational programs using the program PLATO as their basis. Each copy of the program can be used with up to ten students. Each student chooses a password and enters his or her name. The computer then keeps track of individual scores, computed from the answers given to a series of questions.

One program includes questions about the major themes of books in the Bible. The computer prints a question on the computer screen, and the student answers with the name of a book in the Bible. A correct response increases the score. With an incorrect response, the computer explains the correct answer. A question and answer format is used, but the program is designed to reinforce correct answers and provide sufficient review so that the student learns them. This is accomplished through repetition of questions with which the student has difficulty. One strength of this program is that it uses sound educational principles, incorporated into the PLATO educational software.

Smoky Mountain Software of Brevard, North Carolina, has developed a collection of religious education software. One set of these programs creates graphic displays which illustrate Old Testament stories. The pictures are first presented in logical sequence. Then they are mixed up and the student is asked to put them into proper order. The software is so simple to operate that even preschool children can use the program.

Magic Ministry in Dauphin, Pennsylvania, has developed a series of software programs which includes a series of multiple-choice questions on the Gospels of Mark and Luke. The program leads the student through the biblical story, chapter by chapter. This program, like most of those available today, has the questions and answers included as part of the program. In the future we can expect that designers will develop more software that allows the teacher to define the questions asked and the responses expected. Marydel Frohne has written a Bible quiz program which requires the teacher to supply the questions and answers. She has also prepared a tutorial program on the parable of the prodigal son. This program is designed to be a model for students wishing to write their own tutorials on a subject of their choosing.

Hartley Courseware is supplying a program, popular in public schools, called "The Medalist." It has units on states, continents, women in history, and black Americans. Religious educators can examine these programs to understand the educational theory behind the programs and then use a program called "Create Medalist" to design software with a religious content. The "Create" program allows the teacher to pick any topic, select categories, and generate clues.

Six game formats, which can be used with any content material, are available from DLM Teaching Resources. These games are designed to make drill and practice interesting. The documentation is so well written that even a teacher without computer experience can program the individualized content of the games. The games are designed for drill and practice exercises such as vocabulary building and math fact learning, but it would be possible to use them in a religious education setting, in place of or in addition to other methods. For example, in "Idea Invasion," the student is asked to recognize words that fall into a certain category. On the screen, A.O. uses her magic ring to zap invading words which descend from the top of the screen. Students could use this program to practice identifying the names of the twelve disciples, for instance. As names of people descend, A.O. could zap the names of all those who were not disciples.

Group Activities

A computer can present information to a group of children. Cross Educational Software of Ruston, Louisiana, has written a computer program that displays animated pictures on a computer screen to illustrate the story of Jonah. The pictures can be used in a variety of ways. In one form, the pictures appear with the story of Jonah also written on the screen. The story is told in a way suitable for older children or adults.

The story can also be presented with a simplified story line printed on the screen. In this case, not only is the vocabulary simpler, but the letters are much larger, so that younger children can easily read the words. The program advances from one picture to the next when a key is pressed. It is also possible to move backward in the story.

In a third version, only the pictures are displayed on the screen, and the teacher uses the pictures to illustrate the telling of the story. Teachers can choose to use the pictures in a variety of ways. For example, after a lesson on the story of Jonah, the computer-generated pictures could stimulate the students' telling of the story.

In another program available from the same source, the computer displays the words to a hymn. A bouncing ball moves from one word to the next as the computer plays the tune. The program allows both the tempo and pitch of the hymn to be controlled by the user. This program could be used to teach a group of children hymns or just to provide an enjoyable way to sing hymns by having the computer lead the singing.

John Easton has written a program for his church school class at Alterwood United Church in Toronto, Ontario. In this program, the computer first presents the roll. The letter "y" or "n" (for yes or no) must be typed after each name on the list, to indicate whether the student is present. After the list has been completed, the computer counts those who are present and presents the names again. If the computer has the correct number and names, then "y" is entered and the program continues. If an error has been made, the attendance is entered again.

The computer then announces that there will be a quick review of last week's lesson. The first student's name is printed on the screen and a question is asked. If this student types in the correct answer, he or she is rewarded with a cross which flashes across the screen. For an incorrect answer, the computer prints, "That answer is not programmed in my memory," the next student's name is printed on the screen, and the same question given.

If none of the students can answer the question, the first student is asked again, but this time the first letter of the answer is given. If the students still cannot figure out the answer programmed into the computer's memory, more hints are given by providing additional letters, until the complete answer is spelled out.

"Bible Baseball" was written by Chris Tucker of Collegedale, Tennessee. Before the game is played, the teacher must enter fifty questions, with their brief answers, into the computer. Each question is designated as to difficulty: slow, fast, or curve. The students are divided into two teams and take turns at bat. The computer displays a baseball diamond which indicates the position of the runners on the field.

Each batter chooses a question, the computer presents it on the screen, and the batter gives an answer. This is usually typed into the computer, but it can be given orally. When the return button is pressed, the computer displays the answer previously entered into the computer. The umpire must then tell the computer whether the batter has given a correct answer. Since the program is designed to be played with a group, the teacher usually acts as umpire. Students can be given credit for a correct answer, even though it is not the exact answer that is stored in the computer's memory.

A correct answer gives the team a base hit, and an incorrect answer results in a strikeout. After three outs, the second team has a chance to answer questions. The program keeps track of outs and the total score. When each team has had nine turns, the winner is declared.

Fifty new questions could be entered each time the game is played, or only a few new ones could be added each week, covering the material in that week's lesson. Questions from the previous weeks would provide a review.

Teaching Aids

Computers can prepare materials to be used with paper and pencil. Many programs are available, for example, to organize test questions. Testing is not a major concern for most religious educators, but the program could be used to organize questions for computer games or exercises.

A computer program which produces word puzzles would probably be of more use to religious educators. Hi Tech of Santa Cruz, California, has developed three such programs: "Word Search," which produces a puzzle with up to 100 words, in a grid of 5 to 20 rows and columns of letters; "Word Scramble," which produces an anagram puzzle of up to 20 words; and "Word Match," which produces 2 columns of up to 10 words each. The programs are very flexible, allowing the teacher to edit the puzzles by changing, deleting, adding, or relocating the words. The puzzles can be printed on a printer for duplication and use in the classroom.

Word processors also can be used to prepare other materials to be duplicated for use in class. Computers with the ability to produce printed graphics can add interest to classroom materials. In the future we can expect the development of many tools to help teachers with the organization of class materials. Computerized bibliographies and lists of other resources will also make it easier to prepare lessons.

Conclusion

Classroom use of computers for religious education will be determined largely by the issues that have been discussed in this chapter. Will individual computers be available? Will only one computer be available for a group? Will the computer serve only as a teacher's aide? Once the style of computer use has been determined, software can be chosen.

Software designed for one style of computer use may be inappropriate for use with particular hardware. Groups standing around a small screen will not benefit from a program designed for individual use; and software designed for group participation will be effective only when there is a large screen.

Software is written for a specific computer. Each example

of classroom programs given above uses specific hardware. We can expect that software will be available in larger quantities and with increasing quality and utility in the future. But even in the mid-1980s, there are ways to use computers in church school classrooms.

Notes

1. U.S. Congress, House, Committee on Science and Technology, Hearings Before the Subcommittee on Investigations and Oversight, *Computers and Education*, 98th Cong., lst sess., 28, 29 September 1983, No. 64, p. 17.
2. This list was prepared after a helpful conversation with Cheryl Peterson of C-4 Resources.
3. Marydel Frohne, "The Computer in the Church School," *Jed Share* (Summer 1984):27.

CHAPTER FIVE

HOME AND COMMUNITY

T HOUGH it is impossible to predict the impact computers will have on the process of education in the near future, it seems likely that they will encourage and support educational experience outside the classroom. It is possible that the home will become much more important in the field of religious education.

Individualized Study Programs

Computers are well suited to individualized programs of study. As these computers are increasingly present in homes, it will be possible to use them for religious education. Today there is little religious education software available for individualized home study, but such programs probably will be developed in the future.

At first it may seem that home study should not be encouraged because it would result in the isolation of individual Christians. Would it not be better for people to gather at the church for Bible study, rather than for each person to use a computer program at home?

Certainly it is important for Christians to gather for worship, study, and fellowship. But church members who are regular participants in Bible studies also often read Christian literature. Certainly the reading of religious books does not inhibit participation in church activities, and the use of religious education software would be similar to reading a Christian book. Church members will find that time spent at home with a computer program enriches their participation in church-sponsored study programs.

Computer software, like books, will make it possible for individuals to pursue specialized interests. It might be that so few people are interested in a specific topic that it would be impossible to organize a church group. But with computer assistance, that topic could be studied at home.

There are two types of home study with which a computer can be helpful: (1) programs of study that follow a design created by someone else; and (2) research.[1] Home study that follows a course defined by another could take one of several forms. It could be a computerized course, with a tutor who can respond to questions and help interpret results from evaluations. Or one could use software designed for use in a laboratory setting, similar to that described in the last chapter. The software itself provides all tutoring.

Research conjures up the image of large university libraries or dark laboratories. But computers will make it possible for all Christians to have access to vast amounts of information—in some cases on databases accessed over the telephone. But it also will be possible to have computerized libraries right in the home. The computer not only will access this information, but will help organize and sort it so that research can be done effectively. Research really is finding answers to questions, and computers will enable people to find answers quickly and easily.

Computers also can be used at home as word, or idea, processors for journaling. Ideas, questions, and religious experiences can be typed into the machine for a "spiritual" journal. Computerized journals have an advantage over paper journals in that ideas or themes can be reorganized later, or they can be recalled for further reflection. For example, if items are indexed by Scripture and subject, one could quickly find a journal reference to the parable of the good Samaritan entered several years ago. Spiritual journaling has two primary benefits. First, the process of putting ideas into written form helps to clarify those ideas.

Second, recording ideas makes them available for future reference.

Home Religious Education of Children

One of the early experiments with computer-assisted education in a church school setting involved a sex education program which included parental involvement outside the classroom. It was discovered that the computer, providing a neutral source of information, encouraged free discussion of issues between parents and children. Religious education programs which include the presentation of information by a computer may make it possible for the home to be a center of religious education. Religious educators should seriously consider the development of resources for use in homes.

An encyclopedia often makes it possible for parents and children to learn together. Usually a question is the starting point for looking up a fact or figuring out a concept. And in many homes, the encyclopedia is the most complete source of information about religious subjects. The presence of a Bible dictionary, Bible atlas, or Bible commentary is very rare. Most parents do not have enough confidence in their own grasp of Scripture or theological concepts to engage children or other adults in serious dialogue.

But all this can change with the introduction of home computers. These can be connected to a large computer through the telephone line. Whole libraries of material can be consulted; or a video disk with thousands of pages of information can be used. Bringing this educational resource into the home will make it possible for religious education to occur there naturally.

If the home is to become a center for religious education, the church has two projects ahead. Adults must be trained to facilitate the religious education of children in the home, and resources need to be developed.

Software Evaluations

One service religious educators can provide for households is the evaluation of software designed for home use.

There are many ways this service can be organized. Responses and reviews from church members who have purchased particular software packages could be coordinated: Households known to be using home computers can be polled and the educational software they have found useful reported to the congregation. It might be helpful to list the households using specific software, so that other people in the congregation could contact them if they have questions about that particular piece.

A process could be established to examine software designed for home use. A group of people could look at software to determine its ease of use, appropriate age level, and quality of content. This group could also make a subjective judgment about the amount of fun the software provides. The results of these evaluations could be printed for distribution to the congregation.

In the future, denominations may decide to establish software review processes similar to the one established by the National Education Association, described in Chapter 4. But for the present, local churches can provide this service to their members.

Software Lending Library

Some educational software is in the public domain and therefore can be freely copied and distributed. Most religious education software, however, is like church music. The people who created and published it have retained a copyright, and it is illegal to copy, distribute, or use the software without making arrangements with or paying the copyright holder.

If the creator of a particular computer program has given up the right to control its distribution, any church is free to copy the program. Some churches have members who write educational software and who would be happy to share it with their church. In such cases a church library could distribute the software to members.

Software for which the copyright is still in effect can be borrowed from a church software library, as long as the terms of the purchase agreement are followed. Usually this means that only one copy can be used at a time, but other arrangements are possible. Some software purchases include the right to use the software on more than one computer.

Just as a book library makes a wide selection of books available to church members, a church software lending library can increase the diversity of religious education software available to church members. A library of software also makes it possible for members to examine the software before deciding to purchase a particular program.

Informal Learning Centers

Museums and libraries have demonstrated that computers are popular in educational settings in which their use is very loosely structured. The first experiments with informal learning centers were in Boston in the mid-1970s. At the Boston Children's Museum, four terminals were available for playing tic-tac-toe and hang-the-man. At the Lawrence Hall of Science, computer terminals contained programs which composed a simple tune and gave a demonstration of artificial intelligence. These first experiments have mushroomed into thousands of computers and terminals in museums and libraries across the country. Epcot Center at Disney World and Sesame Place in Pennsylvania have been pioneers in making educational computers available in public places. Today public libraries make books available to all people regardless of economic status, but accessibility to computers is limited to people with high incomes.

Through informal learning centers, the church could make computers available to everyone in the community by locating them in a public place. Some churches might also want to provide a more intentional religious education slant by following the pattern of the Christian Science reading rooms. The computers would be supplied with religious education software or have databases of religious education information. The learning center could be promoted in the community as a place where people could study at their own pace, learning about things that interested them.

Computerized Bulletin Boards

With a computer bulletin board, a church can provide information to members and facilitate communication. Once such a board has been set up, members of the church or other interested individuals can telephone a special number. A computer answers the telephone and sends out a beep. When this beep is heard, the person placing the call connects a computer to the telephone line and the two computers can communicate.

Computer bulletin boards serve two primary functions. They provide a way to communicate, and they also provide information. Messages can be left on the host computer in the church for other members, and messages of general interest can be posted for anyone to read. For example, a teacher could leave a message if an emergency made it impossible to be present on Sunday. The advantage of this system is that messages are relayed immediately to the person for whom they are intended, even when that person cannot be contacted directly. The disadvantage is that they work only when people regularly check to see if anyone has left a message for them.

A bulletin board can be a database of information available to church school workers. A library of religious information might be available on the bulletin board for members to use in their homes. Bible handbooks, dictionaries, and commentaries could be available on the bulletin board, to be accessed from home computers.

To set up a bulletin board, a church needs a computer with a modem, special bulletin board software, and a telephone line. The bulletin board could use the church office telephone line and be turned on only when the office is closed. Software for bulletin boards is available for most brands of computers. The purpose of the bulletin board will determine the size disk drive necessary. If it will be used only to exchange messages, then little storage space is necessary. But if it will be used to provide information for the purpose of religious education, the disk will need to be large enough to store large databases. In the latter case, hard disks or some other method of storing large amounts of information will be necessary.

Only members of the church who have computers equipped with modems and software designed for communication could use the bulletin board. Few home computers are now equipped with modems, but it seems likely that as opportunities to obtain useful information through telecommunication increases, more modems will be purchased for home use.

In 1984, United Methodist Communications demonstrated that a denomination can resource the bulletin boards of local congregations. During the United Methodist General Conference, news items were collected, entered into a computer, and then transmitted to several local churches where they were placed on electronic bulletin boards. In this way members had access to the latest information about happenings at the conference.

Church bulletin boards can help sensitize members to the educational potential of large databases. By setting up a local bulletin board with no charges for its use and no long-distance telephone charges, church members can be taught how to use a computer to obtain information. As people become comfortable with the concept, they can begin to use larger and more powerful databases. The availability of large amounts of religious information on computer databases may very well revolutionize religious education, much as did the printing of the Bible.

Notes

1. These two possibilities were suggested by Doug Voss, president of Christian Computer Users Association.

CHAPTER SIX

COMPUTER CLUBS

ORGANIZING a computer club in the church is a sure way to involve people and also to benefit from computers. In this chapter three approaches to computer clubs are discussed: a club where people gather to play games and use computers; a club where people develop computer skills and write games for themselves; and a club where software is developed for the use of others

A Game Club

A church with at least one computer, a collection of religious education software, and a person willing to do a small amount of organizing may find a very positive response to a recreational computer club, where people gather to play games and try out new computer software. Several churches have discovered that a computer has an attraction for youths who had previously resisted other attempts to involve them in the programs of the church.

But a computer club is not only for young people. A Catholic priest in Pennsylvania reported that he had been unsuccessful in developing an adult education program for his parish, although he had tried several approaches. Then he discovered the religious education software developed by C-4 Resources. He uses the software in a club format. Adults are invited to an evening meeting. For the first few minutes of the meeting, the priest talks about the material that will be included in the questions asked by the computer. Then the software is loaded into the computer. As described in Chapter 4, this software provides a sophisticated question and answer session. Just before refreshments are served, a few minutes are spent talking about what people discovered as they used the computer.

If a game club is established for the youth of the church, the sensitivity of the adults who serve as advisors will be as important as the quality of the software. The advisors do not need to be computer experts—it is only necessary to know how to turn on a computer and load software. The more important role for the advisors is to help the youths interpret their learning from the computer games. There will also be opportunities to encourage the development of Christian values.

Although the setting is recreational, a computer club can be a place where religious education occurs. The quality of the software used is certainly important, but a club atmosphere provides a setting where both youths and adults can learn to participate in a Christian community.

A Club That Writes Its Own Software

The best way to really learn something is to teach it, and computers are perfect students. They are predictable and consistent in their responses, and once they are taught something (and it is properly saved on a disk), they never forget and are ready for new learnings. But the person who teaches the computer is also forced to master the material. Real learning can occur when the computer is used as a device to be taught. Teaching a computer is called programming.

All the computer applications discussed in Chapter 4 involved computer software that had been written by someone. A computer club could use any one of those models to write similar software. A computer club could have projects to design graphics presentations of Bible stories. Or a game could be designed to test students' knowledge of characters in the Bible.

It is exciting to write a computer program and then watch it work as expected. An advisor to a computer club need not be an expert computer programmer, because all the members of the club will grow together as programming skills develop. One of the advantages of using a computer-club setting for religious education is that youths can actually see adults struggling to discover solutions. Any computer program can be written in several different ways, so a computer-club setting is an excellent way to provide an experience in which youths can look for their own solutions to a problem, receive support, and experience the fulfillment of reaching a goal.

Although the advisor need not be an expert programmer, it would be helpful if he or she understands enough about the process to be able to identify projects that are beyond the immediate skills of the club. The ability to conceptualize the capabilities of a computer often precedes the ability to actually program the computer to do a task. A club may be excited about using computer graphics to present the life of Jesus, but to program enough graphics screens to tell the story of the whole life of Jesus might take several years. A wise advisor will encourage the club to limit a first project to a presentation of the Easter story.

If members of the club have access to computers at home or in other places, the meetings can be a time to share the results of computer projects, receive feedback and suggestions, and gain ideas about programming. The religious content of the programs can be worked out at club meetings or determined by each individual. One way to provide continuity to the religious education aspect of the club is to focus on a particular area. The missionary journeys of Paul might be used as a theme for a certain period of time: All programs would be designed to explain what Paul said and did, or to test whether Paul's journeys are understood.

A Club That Writes Software for Others

Although the club style described above might result in the production of software that could be used by people outside the club, a club that specifically decides to prepare software for others will take on a somewhat different flavor. In this case the club asks: How can we help the educational program of the church? The club must still define how it will function, but the context will be greater.

The choice of programming projects may involve asking church school teachers what they would find useful. In some cases experimental curriculum could be developed. A club could design a computer-assisted unit for a particular church school class and then actually use the program with that class.

A club that is developing software for the use of the church can involve people who are not interested in the actual programming of a computer, but who can help define the content of the software. A club that helps to resource the educational program of a local church can benefit from the contributions of a wide range of people.

Modifying a Computer Game

There are many books with computer games printed as BASIC program listings. These game programs can by typed into the computer. Some of them can be modified so that before a player can have a turn, a question must be answered correctly. Relatively inexperienced programmers can use this method to create a game to be used for religious education. To illustrate how this might be done, the computer game "Mu-Torere" is shown below.[1] First the BASIC program is listed as it was published in *Big Computer Games.*[2] Then a BASIC listing which could be inserted to require the player to answer a question is shown. This listing could be inserted into "Mu-Torere" or any other program.[3] Three steps must be followed to modify a game:

1. Type a computer game into your computer and make sure it works properly. (Before making any modification, it is important to correct all typing errors, so that the program works.)

2. Find the place in the program where the player is asked to make a response. (This will usually be an INPUT or INKEY\$ statement.) Add a GOSUB statement in this line to a subroutine at the end of the program.

3. Write a subroutine program which requires the correct answer before another turn is allowed. (Further explanation and an example of a subroutine program follow the BASIC program below.)

```
 10 REM **************************
 20 REM * MU-TORRERE *
 30 REM * in Microsoft BASIC *
 40 REM **************************
 50 DEF FN P(X) = X-9*(-1*(X>9))
 60 DEF FN A(X) = A(FN P(X))
 70 DEF FN R(X) = INT(1 + X*RND(1))
 80 GOTO 1030
 90 REM ***Player's Move***
100 PRINT:PRINT:PRINT "Your Move: ";
110 A$ = INKEY$:IF A$ = "" THEN 110
120 PRINT A$;",";:X = VAL(A$)
130 A$ = INKEY$:IF A$ = "" THEN 130
140 PRINT A$:Y = VAL(A$):PRINT
150 IF A(X)<>1 OR A(Y)<>0 THEN 170
160 IF X = 0 OR Y = 0 OR ABS(X-Y) = 1 OR
    ABS(X-Y) = 8 THEN 180
170 PRINT "Invalid move. Try again: ";:GOTO 110
180 A(X) = 0:A(Y) = 1
190 ZR = Y
200 GOSUB 1260
210 P = 1:GOSUB 770:P = -1
220 GOSUB 290
230 IF ZR = Y THEN GOSUB 550
240 A(X) = 0:A(Y) = -1
250 CLS:PRINT " My move: ";:PRINT USING"#";X;:
    PRINT ",";:PRINT USING"#";Y:PF = 1:GOSUB 1150:
    GOSUB 950:GOSUB 770
260 GOSUB 1260
263 REM this line has been added to the original program
    to make the sub routine work better
265 PRINT:PRINT "Press <RETURN> to continue
    game.";:INPUT C$
```

```
270  GOTO 100
280  REM *** Computer's Move ***
290  IF H(1)<>0 THEN H=H(1):GOSUB 660
300  IF SW=1 THEN SW=0:RETURN
310  IF H(2)<>0 THEN H=H(2):GOSUB 660
320  ON (A(0)+2) GOTO 590,340,510
330  REM *** If 0 Square is Empty ***
340  IF FN A(H(2)+8)<>-1 OR FN A(H(2)+1)<>-1
     THEN 370
350  IF FN A(H(2)+7)=-1 THEN X=FN
     P(H(2)+8):Y=0:RETURN
360  IF FN A(H(2)+2)=-1 THEN X=FN
     P(H(2)+1):Y=0:RETURN
370  H(2)=H:IF FN A(H+7)=1 AND FN A(H+8)=-1
     AND FN A(H+1)=1 THEN X=FN P(H+8):Y=-X
380  IF FN A(H+2)=1 AND FN A(H+3)=1 AND
     Y=-X THEN 430
390  IF Y=-X THEN Y=0:RETURN
400  IF FN A(H+2)=1 AND FN A(H+1)=-1 AND FN A(H+8)=1
     THEN X=FN P(H+1):Y=-X
410  IF FN A(H+7)=1 AND FN A(H+6)=1 AND Y=-X
     THEN 430
420  IF Y=-X THEN Y=0:RETURN
430  I=0
440  I=I+1:IF I>9 THEN I=1
450  IF A(I)<>-1 OR FN R(4)<3 THEN 440
460  IF FN A(I+8)=0 AND FN R(4)<3 THEN X=I:
     Y=FN P(I+8):RETURN
470  IF FN A(I+1)=0 AND FN R(4)<3 THEN X=I:
     Y=FN P(I+1):RETURN
480  IF Y<>-I AND FN R(4)<3 THEN X=I:Y=0:RETURN
490  GOTO 440
500  REM *** If 0 Square Contains an X ***
510  H=H(1):GOSUB 690:IF SW=1 THEN SW=0:RETURN
520  H=H(2):GOSUB 690:IF SW=1 THEN SW=0:RETURN
530  IF FN A(H+1)=-1 AND FN R(4)<3 THEN
     X=FN P(H+1):Y=H:RETURN
540  IF FN A(H+8)=-1 AND FN R(4)<3 THEN
     X=FN P(H+8): Y=H:RETURN
550  IF A(0)=-1 AND FN R(4)<3 THEN
     X=0:Y=H(FN R(2)):RETURN
560  IF H=H(2) THEN H=H(1):GOTO 530
570  H=H(2):GOTO 530
```

```
580 REM *** If 0 Square Contains an O ***
590 H=H(1):GOSUB 720:IF SW=1 THEN SW=0:RETURN
600 H=H(2):GOSUB 720:IF SW=1 THEN SW=0: RETURN
610 H=H(1):GOSUB 750:IF SW=1 THEN SW=0: RETURN
620 H=H(2):GOSUB 750:IF SW=1 THEN SW=0:RETURN
630 H=H(1):GOSUB 690:IF SW=1 THEN SW=0:RETURN
640 H=H(2):GOSUB 690:IF SW=1 THEN SW=0:RETURN
650 GOTO 530
660 IF FN A(H+8)=1 AND FN A(H+1)=-1 AND
    FN A(H+2)=-1 THEN X=FN P(H+1):Y=H:
    SW=1:RETURN
670 IF FN A(H+1)=1 AND FN A(H+8)=-1 AND
    FN A(H+7)=-1 THEN X=FN P(H+8):Y=H:
    SW=1:RETURN
680 RETURN
690 IF FN A(H+1)=-1 AND FN A(H+2)=-1 THEN
    X=FN P(H+1):Y=H:SW=1:RETURN
700 IF FN A(H+8)=-1 AND FN A(H+7)=-1 THEN
    X=FN P(H+8):Y=H:SW=1:RETURN
710 RETURN
720 IF FN A(H+8)=-1 AND FN A(H+1)=-1 AND
    FN A(H+2)=0 THEN X=FN P(H+1):Y=FN P(H+2):
    SW=1:RETURN
730 IF FN A(H+1)=-1 AND FN A(H+8)=-1 AND
    FN A(H+7)=0 THEN X=FN P(H+8):
    Y=FN P(H+7):SW=1:RETURN
740 RETURN
750 IF FN A(H+8)=1 AND FN A(H+1)=1 THEN X=0:
    Y=H:SW=1:RETURN
760 RETURN
770 IF A(0)=0 OR A(0)=-P THEN RETURN
780 H=H(1):GOSUB 880:IF Q THEN RETURN
790 H=H(2):GOSUB 880:IF Q THEN RETURN
800 PRINT:PRINT:PRINT
810 BEEP:BEEP:BEEP
820 IF P=1 THEN PRINT "YOU WIN!"
830 IF P=-1 THEN PRINT "THE COMPUTER WINS!"
840 PRINT:PRINT "Care to play again (Y or N) ?";
850 A$=INKEY$:IF A$="" THEN 850
860 IF A$="N" OR A$="n" THEN:CLS:END
870 RUN
880 Q=0
890 IF A(0)=-P THEN Q=1:RETURN
```

```
 900 IF H>1 THEN IF A(H-1)=-P THEN Q=1:RETURN
 910 IF H<8 THEN IF A(H+1)=-P THEN Q=1:RETURN
 920 IF H=1 THEN IF A(9)=-P THEN Q=1:RETURN
 930 IF H=9 THEN IF A(1)=-P THEN Q=1:RETURN
 940 RETURN
 950 H(1)=-1:PRINT
 960 FOR I=1 TO 9
 970 PRINT TAB((4*I-3)+1);
 980 IF A(I)=1 THEN PRINT "X";
 990 IF A(I)=-1 THEN PRINT "O";
1000 IF A(I)=0 THEN PRINT "I";
1010 IF GP=1 THEN RETURN
1020 NEXT I:RETURN
1030 DIM H(2),A(9)
1040 CLS:PRINT TAB(16)"MU-TORERE":PRINT
1050 PRINT " The object of the game is to make it":
     PRINT "impossible for your opponent to move.":PRINT
1060 PRINT " There are 3 types of legal moves:":PRINT:
     PRINT " 1. Sideways to the next adjacent":
     PRINT " square (1 and 9 are adjacent)"
1070 PRINT " 2. To 0 if it is empty":
     PRINT " 3. From 0 to any unoccupied number"
1080 PRINT:PRINT " You and the computer take":
     PRINT " alternating moves until the game ends."
1090 PRINT:PRINT " To move, just press the number you are":
     PRINT "moving from and the number you are":
     PRINT "moving to."
1100 PRINT:PRINT " You play 'X' and the computer":
     PRINT " plays '0'."
1110 PRINT " Press any key to begin.";
1120 A$=INKEY$:IF A$="" THEN 1120
1130 CLS:FOR I=1 TO 4: A(I)=1:A(I+5)=-1:NEXT I
1140 A(0)=0:A(5)=0
1150 PRINT TAB(177)"0":PRINT TAB(17);:GP=1
1160 I=0:GOSUB 980:GP=0:PRINT:PRINT:FOR I=1
     TO 9:PRINT I;" ";:NEXT I
1170 IF PF=1 THEN PF=0:RETURN
1180 GOSUB 950:GOSUB 1260
1190 REM
1200 PRINT:PRINT:PRINT "Do you want to go first (Y or N) ?";
1210 A$=INKEY$:IF A$="" THEN 1210
1220 PRINT:IF A$<>"N" AND A$<>"n" THEN 100
1230 P=-1
```

```
1240  IF FN R(3)<3 THEN A(6)=0:A(5)=-1:X=6:
      Y=5:GOTO 250
1250  X=FN R(4)+5:Y=0:A(X)=0:A(0)=-1:GOTO 250
1260  D=1:FOR I=0 TO 9:IF A(I)=0 THEN H(D)=I:D=D+1
1270  NEXT I:RETURN
```

Careful study of the program listing above shows that the section of the program at which the player is asked for a move is between lines 90 and 180. The second step—finding the exact place at which user input occurs and changing it—is accomplished by a change in line 100 and the inclusion of line 105:

```
100  GOSUB 1280:IF CA=0 GOTO 190
105  PRINT:PRINT:PRINT "Your Move:   ";
```

The third step in writing a subroutine is illustrated below. The numbering of the lines continues from the BASIC program. DATA statements at the end of the program can be changed and expanded to cover any content desired. Any number of DATA statements can be used as long as the final statement is DATA END,END.

```
1280  REM *** Question Area ***
1290  READ QU$,ANS$
1300  IF QU$="END" THEN RESTORE: GOTO 1290
1310  PRINT:PRINT:PRINT QU$
1320  PRINT:PRINT "To earn another turn type correct answer
      in UPPER CASE"
1330  PRINT "and press <RETURN>."
1340  INPUT RES$
1350  IF ANS$=RES$ THEN CA=1:RETURN
1360  PRINT "Sorry that is not the answer the computer has
      been programmed with."
1370  PRINT:PRINT "The answer in the computer is ";ANS$
1380  PRINT:PRINT "Press <RETURN> to continue game.":
      CA=0:INPUT RES$:RETURN
1390  DATA How many commandments did Moses receive,TEN
2000  DATA What is the first book in the Bible,GENESIS
2010  DATA What day is celebrated as Sabbath,SUNDAY
2020  DATA END,END
```

The following illustrations of computer screens show the progress of a game after it has been modified for use in a church school setting. Before attempting to modify a program, test the software to make sure there are no problems with the way it was typed into the computer.

— — — — — — — — — — — — — — —

```
                              O
                              I
1   2   3   4   5   6   7   8   9
X   X   X   X   I   O   O   O   O
```

Do you want to go first (Y or N)?

How many commandments did Moses receive

To earn another turn type correct answer in UPPER CASE and press <RETURN>.
? TEN

Your Move: 2,0

— — — — — — — — — — — — — — —

My move: 6,5
```
                              O
                              X
1   2   3   4   5   6   7   8   9
X   I   X   X   O   I   O   O   O
```
Press <RETURN> to continue game.?

What is the first book in the Bible

To earn another turn type correct answer in UPPER CASE and press <RETURN>.
? MATTHEW

Sorry that is not the answer the computer has been programmed with.

The answer in the computer is GENESIS

Press <RETURN> to continue game.?

— — — — — — — — — — — — — — —

My move: 7,6

```
           O
           X
1  2  3  4  5  6  7  8  9
X  I  X  X  O  O  I  O  O
```

Press <RETURN> to continue game.?

What day is celebrated as Sabbath

To earn another turn type correct answer in UPPER CASE and press <RETURN>.
? SUNDAY

Your Move: 0,2

— — — — — — — — — — — — — — —

My move: 6,0

```
           O
           O
1  2  3  4  5  6  7  8  9
X  X  X  X  O  I  I  O  O
```

THE COMPUTER WINS!

Care to play again (Y or N) ?

— — — — — — — — — — — — — — —

This process is a quick way to develop a collection of games for use in a religious education setting. Adapting a printed game program requires far less programming skill than is required for writing an adventure game.

Writing Adventure Games

Writing an adventure game is a more involved project. But there is potential for the designers of an adventure game to learn a great deal. The resulting adventure also has educational value for the people who play the game.

A computerized adventure game can be designed for any setting. A series of rooms or places are connected according to certain rules. Each room contains objects or clues, and the movement from one room to another is governed by a set of rules. The object of the game is either to collect a set of objects from the rooms or to go through the rooms to reach a certain goal.

Greg Hassett has described the process of writing an adventure game in the chapter "How to Write an Adventure Game," in *Big Computer Games*. Hassett says that the first step is to establish the plot by answering five questions:

> Where will the Adventure take place?
> What will be the main purpose of the Adventure?
> In what kind of world is this supposedly happening?
> What types of obstacles will the player have to overcome?
> How is the player going to get by these obstacles?[4]

In a religious education setting, adventure games could be designed to take place in biblical settings, or in modern settings which raise questions about moral or social issues. An adventure could be designed in which the purpose is to get Abraham from Ur to the land of Canaan. In this case the game designers would need to think about the nature of the world in which Abraham lived: What were the obstacles? How might he have overcome them?

Alternatively, there could be an adventure game in which a church executive wants to provide food for a group of people in a distant land where a flood has destroyed homes and farms. The designers would need to think about the process of church relief work and the difficulty involved in finding resources and delivering aid.

Once the general outline of the adventure has been established, the rooms need to be defined. Adventure games usually have no more than 40 rooms. When the game is played, the player moves from room to room. In some cases, special resources are necessary to move from one room to another. Passwords discovered in one room may be necessary to open a secret door in another room. It is best to write out this design on a large sheet of paper, giving a description of each room and showing the relationship between them. Then the descriptions are entered into the computer.

The third step is to write the program that will interpret the words the player types and control the player's movement through the rooms. This involves a program separating the player's input into a verb/noun combination and comparing the results to a vocabulary table.

Writing these programs involves a moderate level of programming skill. An excellent resource, *Writing Basic Adventure Programs for the TRS-80* by Frank DaCosta, describes how an adventure program can be written using Radio Shack BASIC.[5] The principles can easily be adapted to a computer using another version of BASIC.

Notes

1. Mu-Torere is a game played by the Ngati-Porou tribe in New Zealand. In its original form, the game is played on a nine-pointed star which radiates from a center circle, the *putahi*. The first player places four black stones on four adjacent arms of the star. The second player places white stones at the ends of four adjacent arms. This leaves the center circle and one arm without a stone.

   At any point in the game there are three possible types of moves. A stone can be moved sideways to an adjacent arm if that arm is vacant. A stone can be moved to the center putahi if it is vacant. Or a stone can be moved from the putahi to any vacant arm. Players take turns, and the game is won when a player is unable to make a legal move.
2. David H. Ahl, ed., *Big Computer Games* (Morris Plains, N.J.: Creative Computing Press, 1984). The program was written by Sandy Greenfarb and originally appeared in *Creative Computing* (August 1982).
3. This approach was suggested by Mark Russell.
4. Ahl, *Big Computer Games*, p. 100.
5. Frank DaCosta, *Writing Basic Adventure Programs for the TRS-80* (Blue Ridge, N.J.: TAB Books, 1982).

CHAPTER SEVEN

ADMINISTRATION

M OST church school superintendents would like to spend less time with administrative details so that more could be devoted to people-centered activities. It would be nice if computers could free us from record keeping and report making. But this is an unlikely result of installing a computer. It is more likely that computers will make it possible to use records more effectively and produce reports that are more beneficial. Because records will be used to better advantage, more attention will be given to collecting information that is current and accurate. And better administrative services will result in increased demand for those services.

Ways computers can be used for the administration of religious education are suggested below. These suggestions are based on the assumption that the purpose of church school administration is to provide for the effective use of available resources and to ensure that there are sufficient resources to accomplish the educational goals of the congregation.

A director of religious education or a church school superintendent must evaluate potential computer use by looking at benefits in efficiency, effectiveness, and ability to obtain resources.

Before one plans how to use all the time saved by computer use, one should consider how much time and energy are currently being expended. The total amount of time spent represents the maximum amount of time that might be saved. Many of the tasks of church school administration, however, are not very adaptable to computer assistance. The process of teacher recruitment might benefit from a computer-selected list of those who are likely candidates, but the process of telephoning each individual must be done by a person, not by a computer. An estimate of potential time savings must be limited to looking at those tasks that could be done by a computer.

Increased efficiency may also result in increased effectiveness. If the method of keeping track of telephone numbers is improved so that there are seldom times when a needed number cannot be found, the system is not only more efficient but also more effective.

But increased efficiency does not necessarily result in increased effectiveness. If there is a volunteer who picks out birthday and anniversary cards for all church school participants, puts a short note on each one, and always sends them out a week before the event, the process could be made more efficient with computer-produced address labels. A computer could even be used to generate cards that include individualized messages. Although this system might be much more efficient, it would certainly not be as effective in building fellowship in the church school.

A computer-assisted process can also *decrease* efficiency. If a volunteer counts the attendance in each class and enters the totals on a master sheet, the process of collecting attendance statistics may take less than twenty minutes. Some church software packages are designed so that the name of each person who attends church school must be typed into the computer each week. This task could take more than an hour. If this attendance information is used only to produce total attendance reports, then a task that was previously accomplished in twenty minutes now takes an hour.

It could be argued that although it might take three times as long to type names into a computer than it previously took to count the number of people present, there are additional advantages to having attendance entered into the computer. But each suggested administrative use must be examined very closely. Even if the attendance records that have been computerized will now be used to produce a list of children who have missed three Sundays in a row, the question must be asked: How long would it have taken someone to scan the written attendance sheet to see if anyone had missed three weeks?

An important point to remember is that a computer cannot accomplish any administrative task that could not be accomplished by more traditional methods—typewriter or pencil and paper. The advantage of computers over these traditional methods is that computers can work with large amounts of information very quickly.

Computers will generally be helpful for administrative uses in two kinds of situations: when information will be used many times or in a variety of ways, and when the information needs to be sorted or added. When names and addresses of church school participants are used for mailing lists, when teachers are given lists of class members, when telephone numbers are needed in cases of emergency, or when a church school directory is being prepared, a computer is extremely useful.

In reorganizing and sorting attendance information, a computer is helpful. If attendance is not only counted but average attendance is calculated, minimum and maximum attendance reported, year-to-date attendance calculated, and attendance compared to previous years, a computer will save much time and effort.

There are also times when a computer will be of little help to the administrative function of a church school. If records are kept but reports not made, little benefit will be gained. A list of church school teachers can be kept just as well on a piece of paper as in a computer record, if that list is used only occasionally to find out who is teaching a particular class.

Uses of Computers

Mailing Labels and Phone Lists

A computer is an extremely versatile replacement for an addressograph. Mailing labels can be sorted by the computer in ZIP Code order. Using the ability of the computer to select only certain records, a set of mailing labels can be prepared for any subgroup of the church school. And because the computer uses a master file, addresses can be updated easily; there is no need to change an address in several places.

Computerized mailing lists offer another advantage. Often more than one individual from a household participates in the church school program. There are times when it is nesessary to send a mailing to each individual, but at other times a single mailing to the household will be sufficient and more cost-effective. Although the mailing to a household should be inclusive—"The Williams Family," for instance—the mailing to an individual needs to be clearly personalized. It should not be addressed to "The child of" someone. A properly programmed computer will sort the mailing list, selecting certain addresses and printing the appropriate name on each address label.

In some situations it is better to print directly on the envelopes or sheets of paper. Envelope- and paper-feed devices are available for most printers, so that a series of addresses can be printed without interruption.

Telephone lists are also produced easily by a computer. Accurate lists of telephone numbers still demand careful collection and updating, but the computer's ability to prepare selected lists provides for better use of the information. For example, church school teachers can be provided with a telephone list of all the children in their classes. This makes it more likely that they can contact the students during the week, if they have difficulty finding phone numbers in a directory because they do not know the parents' names.

The computer also facilitates the updating of telephone numbers by automatically changing the records of everyone in that household. It is also possible to keep track of both daytime and evening numbers.

Some people are sensitive about having their unlisted telephone numbers distributed. But the same people want to be called if an event planned for the next day has been cancelled. A computer cannot ensure privacy, but it is possible to have the computer keep track of numbers that are only to be used in an emergency. These numbers can be printed only when an emergency list is desired; they would not be included in a list for general distribution.

Resource and Inventory Management

A church school teacher has been teaching for six months before he discovers that the church has a set of map transparencies for the overhead projector. Two thousand Popsicle sticks are ordered for vacation Bible school, and when they are being put away in the supply closet, it is discovered that there were already three thousand Popsicle sticks there. A large collection of children's books could make a positive contribution to the educational ministry of the church, but the books are too disorganized and there is no check-out system. In each case, a computer could help.

Computers can make lists useful rather than a chore. If lists are entered in the computer and faithfully updated, the information can be obtained in any order. Paper filing systems must have a primary criteria for sorting the information. Books are usually listed by title or author; a second filing system might list them by age level. But consider the teacher who wants a book that has illustrations of Amos. The teacher does not know the title of any such books and does not care what age level the book was written for, since only the illustrations will be used. Even a catalogue by major subject might not provide sufficient information, since a book with illustrations of Amos might be filed under the subject heading "minor prophets." A computerized list which contains the title, author, suggested age level, major subject, and other desired subjects, can be searched by the computer to find a book that meets any criteria. In the case at hand, the teacher could ask the computer for all the books in which Amos is a major or minor subject. If there are a large number, a second search could be made. The computer could be asked for all the children's books with Amos as a subject.

The computer can also help with requests for teaching materials. If all teachers make requests on a standardized form and the requests are entered into the computer, the computer will organize the list so that requests for like materials are combined. If the computer also has a list of sources of supplies, it can match the supplies with the supplier. There will be some situations, however, in which a computer will be of little benefit. It may be easier to look on the shelf in the supply closet to see whether there are any Popsicle sticks. The computer list will be useless unless it is always kept up to date.

Attendance

Some of the issues surrounding the wisdom of using a computer to assist with the recording and reporting of attendance are discussed above. Attendance records may be computerized in order to use them more effectively.

The computer can sort attendance records to identify certain patterns. If students who missed church school for three consecutive weeks were listed, the computer could print a telephone list to be used in contacting those students, or labels for postcards to let the students know they were missed.

Computerized attendance records also can be analyzed very easily. This can be very important both in planning and in evaluating a religious education program. Immediately after someone types attendance into the computer, it can calculate average attendance and compare that day's attendance to the average, or to the attendance in previous years. Thus changing patterns in attendance can be identified.

If a great deal of time is being spent adding or comparing attendance figures, then the computer will be very helpful. Or it will be possible to begin using the attendance information for better administration.

Church School Finances

Whether the expense of a religious education program is part of the church budget and cared for by the church treasurer, or the church school has a separate budget and bank account, a computer can be very helpful.

Commercial accounting software packages or the spreadsheets described below could be used. If the religious education program is part of the larger church budget, it will be important to obtain software that is designed for fund accounting. Not all commercial accounting software is designed for that purpose.

If there are several staff people, a payroll software package is necessary. With payroll software, the computer will calculate pay, figure deductions, and print paychecks. High quality payroll programs will easily handle situations in which there are complicated salary arrangements such as time-and-a-half for Saturdays. At the end of the year the computer adds all deductions and prints W-2 forms and other reports for tax purposes. Before buying a payroll program, one should ascertain that it will work with the state tax laws.

Computerized financial records have the advantage of being able to provide answers to questions. To find how much money has been spent on Popsicle sticks in the last three years, a person using a paper-based system could search through all the records and add the purchases, without being confident that all had been found. A computer could quickly sort through the financial records and find each expenditure for Popsicle sticks. With this information one could decide whether to take advantage of a good price by placing a bulk order for Popsicle sticks, or for any other item.

A computer can also compare expenditures to budget. This is helpful for financial reports, because the computer takes care of adding up all the numbers and making all calculations. But it is also useful to be able to use the computer to look up the current status of expenditures relative to the budget. When a church school teacher asks about purchasing a new record player, the computer can be asked to calculate how much of the equipment budget has been spent thus far. This information will be more up-to-date than the treasurer's most recent finance report.

The computer can print checks for expenditures as well as for payroll. Each expenditure that requires a check can be flagged at the time it is entered, and printed either immediately or at the end of the session. In the best-designed systems, the names and addresses of those who receive checks from the church are kept on a separate computerized list, so that this information does not need to be retyped each time an expenditure is entered. There are printers specially designed to print checks, but any computer printer can be used.

If records of contributions to the religious education program are kept, these can also be computerized. The computer will calculate totals and prepare statements of giving. If certain contributions are not credited to individuals, the income can be entered into the computer as part of the fund accounting system.

Some church school treasurers use a paper spreadsheet to keep track of church school contributions and expenditures. A computer spreadsheet will increase efficiency and accuracy, since the computer will perform all the mathematics.

With financial records (and all other records as well), it is important to keep paper backup copies so that the records can be reconstructed if the information in computer readable form is destroyed. With financial records, this requires software that produces a paper audit trail. A computer with good accounting software will print a record of all transactions after each session. This paper record should be placed in a safe place as insurance against the unlikely occurrence of computer failure or destroyed data.

Scheduling

If a religious education program has only a Sunday church school and an occasional activity, a calendar in the church school office will be adequate for keeping track of all events. But when the program involves complicated scheduling and the physical plant is used by various other groups, then a computer will be of great assistance. If complete information about each event is entered, the computer can check to assure that there are no conflicts. The information also can be used in other ways.

Calendars can be prepared listing all events, or only those of interest to a certain audience. There are church calendar programs that print events in a calendar format. Other programs print lists of events. A calendar of special events for children might be prepared. The list of events can be searched to find specific information. If the date of the last teacher-training workshop is needed, the computer can search for that event and report the date.

The information about scheduling can later be used to evaluate the use of physical facilities or to study whether there is one age group that is receiving insufficient attention in terms of programming.

Newsletters and Promotional Materials

Preparing newsletters, bulletins, and promotional materials usually requires that a staff member type and retype the material until an acceptable copy is prepared for duplicating. Word processing programs, discussed below, will help greatly in producing anything that is now being typed. When documents are written using a word processing program, all corrections and text rearrangements can be made before printing. Some printers will even cut mimeograph stencils. Offices with dry paper copiers can use the computer-printed page as the original.

A word processor also can be used to set type for printed materials. Some commercial printers will accept computer-generated text and convert it into type. This can be done by delivering a floppy disk to the printer or by sending the information over telephone lines, using a modem. If the text is prepared at the church, there is better control. Any mistakes in the final copy would have been made in the church office, not by the printer.

Because word processing makes it easier to produce written material, administrators can spend more time creating promotional materials and less time working on the production of those materials.

Some documents can be prepared more quickly, since previous documents can be modified rather than being completely retyped. The agenda for a monthly programming committee may change very little from month to month. With a word processor the previous month's agenda is modified, the date changed, and a new agenda printed.

Names, addresses, and other information can be inserted into letters or other documents. This makes it possible to personalize communications. A letter announcing the beginning of a fall church school program can be individually addressed to each child. The letter also can contain the name of the child's new teacher and which room the class will be using. The computer will look up all this information and insert it into an otherwise standard letter.

Dot matrix printers can be used to produce fancy certificates of attendance or promotion. These certificates can be specifically designed so that each is unique.

Administrative Software

There is software specifically designed to help with the administration of a church school. The advantage of using this software is that no thought needs to be given to ways the computer will be used. Information is entered into the computer according to the rules established by the people who wrote the software, and reports are generated using that information.

But this advantage may turn out to be a disadvantage. Because the software was designed to be used in many settings, it will not necessarily address the specific administrative needs of a particular situation. A system that is good for most churches may not be exactly what is needed in your church school.

As an alternative to using software designed for church schools, most administrators will find that commercial business software—word processing, database management, and spreadsheet software—can easily be adapted to meet their needs.

Word processing software can be used to produce any document that is usually written or typed. The primary advantage of using a word processor rather than a typewriter is that corrections and revisions can be made easily. Words can be changed or reorganized on the screen before they are printed on paper. Most word processing programs will produce personalized letters or notices. WordStar and Paper Clip are examples of word processing software.

Database management software is designed to help with the management of lists. Information is entered into the computer, using a form usually designed by the user. The administrator who designs the system decides what information is necessary and provides a place for it on the *form* that appears on the screen. The information collected on each copy of the form is called a *record*. If the database is being used to keep track of registration in church school, the information about each student would be a record. All the records made by filling in a particular form are called a *file*. So the computer would keep a file of the church school registration.

List management software can be used with only one file at a time. With most list management software packages it is possible to look up records to satisfy a particular requirement. For example, one could generate a list of all the children who live on Pine Street. Both PFS File and Perfect Filer are list managers.

Relational databases do the same things list managers do, but they are not limited to one file at a time. The information in one file can be looked up and used while another file also is being used. This is very useful if there is only one computer for both church school administration and the church office. The file with the names of children enrolled in the church school can be related to the file of addresses of households in the church. When an address is corrected for a church member, it will be updated automatically on the church school record. DBase III and Condor are relational database programs.

List management database programs use the information in any one file to generate reports. Common reports include mailing labels, directories, and class lists. Each report will present selected parts of the information kept in the record. The report will also sort records and present them in a particular order. Mailing labels would be sorted in ZIP Code order. Some reports might select only certain records.

Relational databases can produce reports which use information from several files. A report might first sort the household records into alphabetical order, then select those that have no record of attendance in the attendance file, then print the names of the children, and finally, the teacher for their age group from the file which contains teachers' names. This report could be used to identify children to be contacted.

A spreadsheet is similar to a database, in that it is a way to list information—the information is entered and presented in rows and columns. Spreadsheets are particularly useful for numbers, because the computer can reorder the items in a row or column, add a series of numbers, or perform other mathematical functions. The spreadsheet is like a paper spreadsheet, except that the computer makes it possible to manipulate the information.

A spreadsheet might be used to keep track of attendance at church school. The names of the classes would be listed down the left side of the spreadsheet and the dates of Sundays across the top. The attendance for each class would be entered below the date and opposite the class name. At the bottom of the spreadsheet the computer would calculate the total attendance for each Sunday, and average attendance for each class could be calculated and displayed.

The computer keeps track of information as if it were a very large paper spreadsheet. The user can view parts of the large spreadsheet by instructing the computer to move from one section to another. With a relational spreadsheet, the total attendance for each week could be moved to another spreadsheet, where only a summary would be presented. Whole spreadsheets or selected portions can be printed onto paper.

Integrated applications software combines the characteristics of word processing, database management, and a spreadsheet. Information can be entered in the computer by typing it into a form. Later, this might be combined with other information and presented in rows and columns in spreadsheet format. The spreadsheet presentation can be used as part of a report written with the word processing capabilities of the software. Symphony and Framework are examples of integrated applications software.

Equipment for Administration

What equipment will be needed to accomplish all this? For the administrative tasks discussed above, software is available for almost any computer, from the Commodore 64 to the IBM PC or Apple MacIntosh. One computer may sort a mailing list a little more quickly. Another will have software that is a little easier to use. But for the most part, the choice of computer hardware is a matter of taste, combined with budget constraints. It is a little like buying an automobile. Any car will get you from one place to another, but individuals still express strong preference for one model over another.

The selection of an off-line storage device and a printer is more difficult. Off-line storage devices differ in their capacity to store information, and in their speed. A cassette recorder can be eliminated for administrative use—it is slow and very difficult to use with large amounts of information. In an administrative situation, a hard disk drive may be necessary because it is much faster and stores more information than other devices. But most churches will find that floppy disks are sufficient and the most cost-effective method of storing information.

To gain a sense of how much information is used in your religious education situation, think of the information used by the computer in the same way you think of information written on paper. A single-spaced typewritten page contains about three thousand characters. Computer manuals use the words *byte* rather than *character* and *K* rather than *thousand*. So an off-line storage device needs to have about 3K of space to store one typewritten page.

Now think about the amount of information that is kept (or is likely to be kept if a computer is used). If 260 people are registered in the church school and about one-fifth of a page of information is kept for each person, then there will be a need for 156K of disk storage. Floppy disk drives come in different sizes. In this case, any disk drive that will store at least 160K on a disk will be sufficient. Similar calculations can be done to estimate the size disk drive necessary for other applications, such as the inventory of church school supplies. If the amount of information exceeds the amount of material that can be stored on a single floppy disk, it is possible to use more than one disk. Half the information would be on one disk and the other half on another. When the computer is sorting through the data, the two disks must be inserted into the disk drive one after another, so that the information is available to the computer. Although this is possible, it is not recommended. When the amount of information that will be used for a single application exceeds the amount that can be stored on one disk, it is best to consider using a hard disk.

Hard disks commonly store ten, twenty, or thirty million bytes. Twenty million bytes contain more than six thousand pages of information. Administrative uses of a computer for religious education are not likely to demand more off-line storage than is available on a hard disk.

Another way to increase the amount of information available to the computer at one time is to have two or more floppy disk drives. With two disk drives, it is easier to make a copy of a disk. The computer can quickly move information from one to another. This is called making a backup, an extremely important precaution to insure that information is not lost.

A printer will usually be necessary. Dot matrix printers produce letters by printing a series of dots across the page; the copy looks as if it were generated by a computer. The advantage of these printers is that they are usually inexpensive and very fast. There are also printers which produce copy that looks as if it were typed. These letter-quality printers are usually slower than dot matrix printers. If large amounts of information will be printed each week, the speed of the printer is very important.

Chapter 3 described several alternative methods of obtaining a computer. It is very likely that the computer used for other administrative purposes in the church can also be used for religious education.

CHAPTER EIGHT

THE
SOCIAL
CONTEXT
OF COMPUTERS

THE computer is usually presented as a tool of the future. From this perspective, it is reasonable to ask whether there will be any psychological side effects from the widespread penetration of computer education. As noted in the first chapter, this question is of particular interest to religious educators because they have struggled with issues concerning the relationship of method and content. They will ask whether using a computer will contradict the content being presented. Can we expect that children who use computer-assisted education will be more likely to develop certain values than those who do not? And if the use of computers encourages the adoption of certain values, are those values consistent with the goals of religious education?

Even the church that decides not to use computers needs to be sensitive to the impact computers are having on church members. Computers can be considered from either of two perspectives: (1) Accept computers as cultural givens—technical tools that are part of the environment in which religious education is conducted; (2) view computers as both a product of and a contribution to the value system that exists in the society.

The first approach, typified by the person who says, "Computers are just tools that can be used or not used," has limited usefulness, because computers are a part of the profound changes in society. They create new opportunities and, therefore, the need for new responses. By assuming that computers are a cultural given, the first approach overlooks the influence of the value system which supported the invention and spread of computers. Religious educators must deal with that value system, even though computers are rejected as tools for religious education. The psychological approach to evaluating the impact of computers suffers from the assumption that they are simply a part of the human environment. Yet religious educators will want to look carefully at the findings of those who are conducting psychological research.

The second perspective is adopted here. It is argued that it is possible to understand the development of personal computers as an expression of values. At one level, this means that each computer designed reflects a paticular set of values. At a more profound level, the roots of the changes going on in society can be seen in the development of values, some of which were fully expressed in the late nineteenth and early twentieth centuries. These new values can be summarized as professionalization, the objectification of knowledge, and the acceptance of artifical intelligence. The potential use of computers for religious education can most fruitfully be considered within the context of recognizing the cultural value system which has supported computers.

The Psychological Approach

Many of the questions concerned with the impact of computers are a natural outgrowth of our experience with television. Only recently have psychologists seriously begun to study the effects of massive exposure to television. Of particular concern is the increase in violence in society that has accompanied increased exposure to television. Studies have been based on a suspicion that the violent content of commercial television encourages viewers to participate in violent acts.

If violent television programs cause children to be violent, and programs that model cooperative social behavior cause children to value cooperation, then society's experience with television provides a simple lesson. Before computers become widely used, care must be taken to ensure that the content of computer education software is based upon a model of cooperative, rather than violent social interaction. But life is never so simple. The psychological impact of television is not understood even now, after television has become common in American homes. And any predictions about psychological effects of computers are extremely problematic.

The first attempts to define computers' effect on children have been inconclusive. Sherry Turkle has observed children's reactions to computers.[1] She says there are two styles of response: hard mastery and soft mastery. The first is the approach of the engineer; the second is that of the artist. Turkle offers the warning that we must be careful not to impose the hard mastery approach on the natural development of every child.

Craig Brod has presented a far more frightening picture. He says there is

> a new kind of disease: Technostress. Technostress is a modern disease of adaptation caused by an inability to cope with the new computer technologies in a healthy manner. It manifests itself in two distinct but related ways: in the struggle to accept computer technology, and in the more specialized form of over-identification with computer technology.[2]

According to Brod, adults are not the only victims of this disease.

> Children today are weathering the same cultural forces as electronic office workers. Despite the self-congratulatory tone of most computers-and-kids stories in newspapers and magazines and PTA bulletins, technostress is becoming a factor in even young children. Many computer-involved youngsters suffer from the same mental strain, alteration of time, tyranny of perfection, mechanical social relations, and isolation that technostressed adults experience.[3]

Even Brod's description of what is happening to some individuals is not really related to psychology. It is a description of changes occurring in the society. Because computers are a social phenomenon, a consideration of their impact should begin by looking at what is happening in the society.

A Changing Society

Computers are only a part of a social transformation that is all-encompassing. As Alexander King wrote in the introduction to *Microelectronics and Society:*

> We are entering a period of deep transition which may last from thirty to fifty years before leading to a completely different type of world society with much greater numbers, changed values, new political and administrative structures, entirely novel forms of institutional behavior and a technological basis very different from what we are familiar with today, which will influence lifestyles fundamentally in all nations and all cultures.[4]

Alvin Toffler had made the same point earlier, in *The Third Wave:* "What is happening now is nothing less than a global revolution, a quantum jump in history."[5] Fritjof Capra says, "The current crisis, therefore, is not just a crisis of individuals, governments, or social institutions; it is a transition of planetary dimensions. As individuals, as a society, as a civilization, and as a planetary ecosystem, we are reaching the turning point."[6]

The term *postindustrial society* was coined by Harvard sociologist Daniel Bell to describe the period of history he believes has already begun. The use of computers and telecommunications has made it possible to think about a postindustrial society. The religious education use of computers must be considered in this context.

Is religious education relevant in this changing world? Should religious educators join the worldwide cultural revolution? Or does the religious community need to refrain from participating in some of the changes that are taking place? To what extent are the changes determined by technology? Will the educational practices of the church influence the direction of cultural changes in the near future?

Our difficulty in answering these questions lies in the fact that the context within which they must be considered involves very fundamental issues. Ultimately, the consideration of computer use leads us to questions about the nature of reality, the role of society, and the nature of God. It would be nice if we could put all these issues aside and just talk about screen resolution, necessary memory, and passive versus interactive presentations. It would be nice if computer technology could be thought of as just another educational tool, like a chalkboard or a flannelgraph.

But computers are not just something that happened to come along. There have been years of cultural and technical preparation. In 1976, Joseph Weizenbaum observed that "we, all of us, have made the world too much into a computer, and that this remaking of the world in the image of the computer started long before there were any electronic computers."[7] It is tempting to think of computers as just another tool, an advancement over previous tools. But they are much more. Computers represent a way of looking at reality.

Computers as a Defining Technology

Computers in today's world are what J. David Bolter calls a "defining technology":

> Continually redrawing the line that divides nature and culture, men have always been inclined to explain the former in terms of the latter, to examine the world of nature through the lens of their own created human environment. So Greek philosophers used analogies from the crafts of pottery and woodworking to explain the creation of the universe: the stars, the planets, the earth, and its living inhabitants. In the same way, the weight-driven clock invented in the Middle Ages provided a new metaphor for both the regular movements of heavenly bodies and the beautifully intricate bodies of animals, whereas the widespread use of the steam engine in the nineteenth century brought to mind a different, more brutal aspect of the

natural world. It is certainly not true that changing technology is solely responsible for mankind's changing views of nature, but clearly the technology of any age provides an attractive window through which thinkers can view both their physical and metaphysical worlds.[8]

Bolter goes on, "Today the computer is constantly serving as a metaphor for the human mind or brain: psychologists speak of the input and output, sometimes even the hardware and software, of the brain; linguists treat human language as if it were a programming code; and everyone speaks of making computers 'think.' "[9] Every defining technology has had clear implications for the religious community, but the computer is particularly challenging. Unlike a Greek pot, a clock, or a steam engine, a computer can be used for religious education. And people living in a computer culture will have particular ways of looking at the world.

Religious educators need to recognize that the questions, interests, and acceptable evidence or arguments designed for people who accept the computer as the defining technology will not be exactly the same as those designed for people whose defined technology was the steam engine. Even in situations where computers are not actually used, they will have an influence.

The Computer as an Expression of Values

Before the computer could become a defining technology, it was necessary for individual computers to be invented. They needed to become common objects throughout the society.

Computers can be viewed as expressions of the values of the people who create them—and their reception by the public can be seen as a reflection of the values within a subgroup of the population. This is illustrated by looking at several commercial computers.

The Apple II was designed by people who thought of the computer as an exciting tool for the hobbyist. It contained slots for the addition of hardware, and the manuals included complete technical information, describing how the computer worked and suggesting ways to take full advantage of its capabilities. The Apple II has been very popular with a group of people who not only want to be able to use a computer, but also want to learn what computers are all about.

The TI 99/4 was designed by engineers at Texas Instrument Corporation, a major manufacturer of computer chips, the primary component of personal computers. The company has also been a leader in the development of inexpensive hand-held calculators. The computer they designed contained an extremely advanced computer chip, and its keyboard was an enlarged calculator keyboard. The TI 99/4 could be used as a very sophisticated calculator. This computer expressed the values of people who loved calculators and liked making sophisticated computer chips. Not as many people were excited by the TI 99/4 as by the Apple II. It turned out that the calculator mentality did not extend far beyond Texas Instrument's own staff.

The PC Jr., from computer giant IBM, offers an interesting example of a computer product that failed. The PC Jr. was extremely popular. It captured a larger share of total computer sales during its first year than any other inexpensive computer. At its peak, it rivaled the Apple II. With the PC Jr., IBM appeared to have designed a machine that fit the values of a large group of people. They wanted a computer that was powerful, boasted a large software library, was relatively inexpensive, and carried a prestigious label.

Although IBM had a product people were buying, its manufacture was abruptly stopped. The reason: In the past, IBM had controlled the mainframe market by leasing rather than selling equipment, thus ensuring dependence on IBM for support. Although the PC Jr. was popular with the public, it was impossible for IBM to exercise sufficient control over the market, so the product was discontinued.

If computers are a reflection of the values of the people who design them, and their success or failure in the marketplace is also related to value systems, then we should look at a computer not as a tool, but as a work of art. Today we visit a museum to view the beautiful drawings on ancient pottery. They are interesting to us because they tell us about the people who used the pottery. We value a Greek vase because of its artistic qualities, but sometimes forget that it also had a very utilitarian purpose.

Similarly, future generations will be able to look at the computers we have produced and chosen to use, appreciating the fact that these machines are expressions of what was important to us. Computers have been designed by individual people, and they are purchased by individuals. But just as Greek vases are expressions of Greek culture, computers also are expressions of culture.

Cultural Roots of Technology

Why were computers developed in the first place? What were the underlying values or social forces that resulted in the invention and use of computers? If religious educators are to examine the use of computers critically, then it is essential to look at their cultural roots.

Because invention of the computer would have been impossible without the industrial revolution, it is necessary to first consider the cultural changes that made machines possible. Lewis Mumford attempted to understand the coming of the industrial revolution by searching for cultural preparation. At that time, human society changed from tool dependency to machine dependency. But for Mumford, the invention of the machine was not sufficient to account for its acceptance and application: "Before the new industrial processes could take hold on a great scale, a reorientation of wishes, habits, ideas, goals was necessary."[10]

In 1930, Mumford worried about a future in which "the machine ceases to be a substitute for God or for an orderly society; and instead of its success being measured by the mechanization of life, its worth becomes more and more measurable in terms of its own approach to the organic and the living."[11] Computers had not yet been invented, but

Mumford saw the postindustrial society coming. His analysis of the cultural developments which surrounded the introduction of machines is helpful: It shows us the cultural changes which set the stage for computers and also provides a model for studying the more recent changes which preceded them.

In his chapter "Cultural Preparation" in *Technics and Civilization*, Mumford presents a list of cultural developments that prepared the way for the industrial revolution. Three of these—the monastic movement (and the clock), the altered perception of labor as something that could be exchanged for money (labor was objectified), and the removal of spirit from objects—are particularly interesting because each has a parallel in the cultural changes which preceded the postindustrial age.

During this century the professions have provided a new model for vocation, just as monasticism did in the thirteenth. The objectification of money and the beginnings of capitalism in the twelfth and thirteenth centuries are paralleled by the objectification of information and knowledge in recent years. And the success of western Christianity in removing the spirit from objects by destroying belief in animism has been paralleled in recent times by the introduction of a concept of artificial intelligence. The fact that artificial intelligence is taken seriously illustrates that a fundamental change has occurred. In previous ages, the very idea of an intelligence that was not a part of human consciousness would have been unthinkable.

Because the computer would have been impossible without the industrial age, our understanding of the cultural preparation for the computer will benefit from a review of Mumford's arguments in regard to these three preparations for the industrial revolution.

Preparations for the Industrial Age

The monastic movement dates from the third century and has roots in even earlier Christian, Jewish, and Greek communities. But the thirteenth century saw the Christian monastic movement mature. As Clyde Manschreck points out, "The thirteenth century marked the predominance of the church in Western culture. . . . Never before had the church enjoyed such preeminence."[12] The Dominicans were founded in 1214, and the Franciscans were approved by the Pope in 1210.

Originally serving to support the institutional church, the ordered life became valued in its own right. The movement from monastery to factory was natural. Even those who had never been inside a monastery lived in a society where the best life was an ordered life. The clock and other machines were valued because they represented order. Thus monasticism was important in preparing the way for the invention and use of machines.

Borrowing from the ideas of Karl Marx, Mumford points out that in the fourteenth century, international exchange of money began. Money makes it possible to convert the value of any tangible or intangible item into a common denominator, so that it can be sold or purchased. Money itself became a commodity, distinct from the labor or objects for which it was exchanged. Mumford writes,

> This last fact was particularly important for life and thought: the quest of power by means of abstractions. One abstraction reinforced the other. Time was money; money was power; power required the furtherance of trade and production: production was diverted . . . toward the acquisition of larger profits, with a larger margin for new capital expenditures for wars, foreign conquests, mines, productive enterprises . . . more money and more power.[13]

Objectification is a difficult concept for people living in the twentieth century to understand because we have been so culturally conditioned to accept the idea that we live in a world with material reality and that even things that are clearly not material can be given an equivalent value in money. It seems obvious to us that a songwriter can sell a song or that physical work can be exchanged for money. But this worldview is not universal to all cultures and has developed in western civilization just since the Middle Ages.

Only as the culture adopted an understanding of money which allowed it to be converted into labor or creative products, could machines take a central place in social organization. Both machines and people could contribute a monetary equivalent to production. Changing understandings within the culture about money and labor prepared the way for the widespread use of machines.

The third cultural preparation for the industrial age identified by Mumford is the removal of spirit from objects—the end of animism. This relates to the previously discussed attempts by the Christian church to establish control over European society. Anselm of Canterbury (1070–1121), also a defender of the authority of the Pope, is most famous for establishing ontological proof of the existence of God. Afterward, theologians struggled for several hundred years with the problems raised by the transfer of God from empirical experience into a logical category.

William of Champeaux, Roscellinus of Compiegne, and Peter Abelard were all predecessors of the scholastic theologians in the early thirteenth century who discovered the logic of Aristotle and proposed a theology that separated the supernatural world from the world governed by logic. Thomas Aquinas, a Dominican, presented these arguments in *Summa Theologiae*.

Aquinas stated that theology examines the supernatural, which is the province of God and the church: While we can have knowledge about the material world, it is only through revelation that we can know about God, and the church plays a central role as the receiver, preserver, and propagator of revelation. While the original function of scholastic theology was to legitimize the position of the church, one of its important effects on society was the removal of the spiritual dimension from all objects. Mumford points out:

> The meaning of this division did not fully become apparent until the Schoolmen themselves had fallen into

111

disrepute and their inheritors, like Descartes, had begun to take advantage of the old breach by describing on a purely mechanical basis the entire world of nature—leaving out only the Church's special province, the soul of man.[14]

Today the objectification of nature is so obvious that it is difficult to imagine that it is only recently that people have been freed to think of objects as material, with no spiritual dimension. Mumford reminds us:

> The specific triumph of the technical imagination rested on the ability to dissociate lifting power from the arm and create a crane; to dissociate work from the action of men and animals and create the water-mill; to dissociate light from the combustion of wood and oil and create the electric lamp. For thousands of years animism had stood in the way of this development; for it had concealed the entire face of nature behind a scrawl of human forms. . . . Life, not content with its own province, had flowed incontinently into stones, rivers, stars, and all the natural elements.[15]

Today we think of machines as physical objects which are completely predictable and can be controlled by us if we understand them. But people who see spirits in all objects could not take this attitude. The large scale introduction of machines into society could have happened only after the destruction of animism. An auto mechanic who believes there is an unpredictable spirit within each car engine would not be able to repair cars with much confidence.

Mumford points to several additional cultural changes which paved the way for the acceptance of machines and the industrial revolution, but those we have mentioned are of special interest here because they parallel the cultural changes that have preceded computers. Just as monasticism provided a new model for life-style, professionalism has defined the desired modern life-style. The objectification of information parallels the previous objectification of labor, and the concept of artificial intelligence is an idea as profound in its cultural implications as was the end of animism. These three recent cultural changes are discussed below.

The Ideology of Professionalism

The rise of professionalism has played a role similar to that of monasticism. Magali Sarfatti Larson has studied the beginnings of professionalism and documented its emergence during the last hundred years: "Viewed in the larger perspective of the occupational and class structures, it would appear that the model of profession passes from a predominantly economic function—organizing the linkage between education and the marketplace—to a predominantly ideological one, justifying inequality of status and closure of access in the occupational order."[16]

According to Larson, the ideology of professionalism includes a belief in the intrinsic value of work, the ideal of universal service, and a status model wherein high rank imposes duties. These themes are not newly introduced into the dominant ideology, but are "carried, from a traditional past, the liberal phase of capitalism, into the division of labor of the monopolistic phase."[17] The innovation in the ideology of professionalism is the role of knowledge, information, and education credentialing.

Today a useful and fulfilled life is defined as that of the professional. It is not only doctors, but nurses and plumbers who want to be professionals. They want standards established, and they want limits placed on the people permitted to practice their professions. The new culturally instilled goal of all individuals, from lawyers to parking-lot attendants, is to act in a professional way. The ideology of professionalism is complicated, but a central feature is that the professional is a person who exercises judgment. The rationale for requiring education, and for limiting those who can practice, is that some care must be taken that professionals exercise good judgment.

The computer is, in many ways, the embodiment of the ideology of professionalism. John Kemeny, the president of Dartmouth College and an early promoter of computers in educational settings, has written about the day he first heard a modern computer suggested:

> In 1949 I had the privilege of listening to a lecture at Los Alamos by the great Hungarian-born mathematician John von Neumann [who] proposed that we should be able to store a set of instructions within the internal memory of the machine so that the computer could go from step to step by consulting its own memory without waiting for human interference.[18]

The vision was to have a machine that would consult its own resources to act in a professional way. Not only Kemeny, but the whole society was excited by a machine that would be professional.

As religious educators evaluate the implications of computers, it is necessary to reflect on the cultural preparation supplied by the ideology of professionalism. Are the values of this ideology consistent with Christian values? Professionalism functions to limit access to certain positions and privileges. How does this fit with the message of the gospel? Even if computers are not used in a religious education program during church school, religious educators must struggle with this effect of the changing cultural values that has preceded and accompanied their use.

Objectification of Knowledge

Before computers could be fully accepted, knowledge and information needed to be objectified, just as money had objectified labor and the products of industry. Only recently has it become possible to think of information as a commodity that can be collected, traded, and even sold for money.

Codifying human understanding is not a new activity. Only because of written records are we able to know very much about ancient civilizations. Those records include lists of possessions and transactions, lists of rulers and conquests, and sacred writings. These naturally led to the codifying of relationships in the form of laws and descriptions of the way the gods related to people. Both the Greeks and the Romans wrote encyclopedias.

But the last hundred and fifty years have witnessed a

profound change in society's understanding and use of information and knowledge. Our difficulty today in obtaining an "accurate" text of the Bible illustrates that present-day attitudes toward information are very different from the attitudes of people in the past. While some "corruption" of biblical texts is due to careless mistakes of scribes who copied them, other "problem" variations in the oldest texts available to us are the result of changes made because people thought they were clarifying, or harmonizing, or improving the words.

Just over two hundred years ago, John Wesley freely edited the religious classics before printing them for distribution to his followers. When he sent the Apostles' Creed to Methodists in America, he even changed the words in that ancient statement of faith. Today an editor would be more concerned about preserving the original words of religious classics, because information has become objectified. But in the not so distant past, to correct a word, or even to change an idea, was not to corrupt a text. The text was not thought of as having a reality of its own. It was not objectified.

The history of encyclopedias illustrates the objectification of knowledge. During the first sixteen centuries of encyclopedia production, it was a document that reflected the editors' attempt to present information that mirrored the resources available. These anthologies were freely edited and organized around the material at hand. As late as 1435, Alfonso de la Torre organized his encyclopedia using the allegorical approach of a child receiving instruction from a series of maidens—Grammar, Logic, Rhetoric, and so on. We know of a second-century encyclopedia, prepared by Sextus Pompeius Festus, arranged in alphabetical order. *Suidas* is a tenth- or eleventh-century encyclopedia-dictionary arranged alphabetically, but it seems to have had little influence on future encyclopedias. We might wonder why those who prepared encyclopedias knew about alphabetical organization, yet chose not to use that method. The answer is that their understanding of knowledge was very different from ours. It did not occur to them that information is a commodity which can be put into order and organized for distribution.

Francis Bacon is credited with conceiving a new plan for encyclopedias. His unfinished *Instauratio Magna* (1620) is a bridge between ancient and modern encyclopedias. As his title indicates, he viewed his work as a great restoration. It did not include the controversies found in literature, but codified knowledge in an authoritative presentation, even including a checklist to insure that nothing had been left out. Knowledge was something that could be listed completely.

After Bacon, the role of encyclopedias changed. Now the purpose was to make knowledge available to individuals, but alphabetical ordering of entries was not yet standard. As recently as 1817, Coleridge's *Encyclopaedia Metropolitana* used an organization similar to Bacon's. He argued that this would "present the circle of knowledge in its harmony" and give a "unity of design and of elucidation." But the practice of using alphabetical order to present the material triumphed, because the culture viewed knowledge not in its "harmony," but in its objectified form.

In 1768 the encyclopedic tradition reached maturity with the publication in Scotland of the first edition of *Encyclopaedia Britannica*, a comprehensive collection of articles written by a group of people who attempted to report all knowledge as it was then known. Its organization was specifically designed to make it easy for the reader to find information. The 1922 edition marked the triumph of the objectification of knowledge. For that edition, the editors asked experts in every field to prepare credited articles. It was no longer necessary for encyclopedia articles to remain anonymous to indicate their authority. Knowledge had become so objectified that signed articles did not suggest the contrary.

The computer is specifically designed to use information that has been objectified—only unambiguous information can be manipulated in a meaningful way. The objectification of knowledge was a necessary cultural preparation for computers. Most religious educators have accepted this objectification of knowledge, but serious questions are raised when religious knowledge is objectified. An evaluation of the proper role for computers must reflect on the nature of religious knowledge and the cultural attitudes toward knowledge.

Artificial Intelligence Accepted

Whether it is possible to create the equivalent of intelligence in a computer is discussed in the next chapter. But even if it turns out that there is something about intelligence that cannot be duplicated by a machine, the concept of artificial intelligence has made it possible for society to conceive of and develop computers. This concept is closely linked to the process of professionalization and the objectification of knowledge. All are part of the redefinition of cultural values which has occurred during the past two hundred years.

The concept of artificial intelligence presents a challenge to religious educators. If machines are capable of intelligence, what implications does that have for religious education? Is it the goal of religious educators to teach people something a machine cannot learn? Is there anything that could not be taught by or to a machine?

Conclusion

We began this chapter with a consideration of whether computers would have a psychological effect on the children who use them. But as we have seen, computers have become part of the culture, in conjunction with profound changes in cultural values. The people who use computers are different from people who lived two hundred years ago. Those changes were not caused by the computer, but were part of the cultural changes which prepared the way for computers.

Religious educators cannot plan for the use of computers without considering the value system from which they have sprung. The questions raised are primarily theological rather than methodological, but they can be phrased in terms of using computers for religious education: Should the use of computers be professionalized, with standards established, and certification of those qualified to use the new tools? Can the content of religious education be objectified? Will artificial intelligence allow educators to use new and better methods of teaching religion?

Even if the cultural values that have surrounded and encouraged the invention and use of computers are contrary to Christian values, it may be possible to redeem the computer from its cultural roots. Once a technology is developed, it need not remain tied to the ideology and values that encouraged its development. An example of this is the stirrup, which was introduced into Europe and became a central technology for the establishment of feudalism. With the stirrup, it was possible for a small group of soldiers on horseback to defeat large armies of foot soldiers, so that feudal lords were able to defend their territories. Although the technology was developed hundreds of years before in China, its large-scale application grew out of the values of a feudal society. In another cultural setting, the stirrup had less negative social consequence: Using the same technology, ranchers in the American Southwest managed large herds of cattle.

Even if the church must pronounce a negative judgment on the cultural values that have promoted the development of computers, there may be ways the technology can be used constructively. But if computers are not going to draw the church into supporting the values that have prepared their way, then very serious theological work will be necessary. Religious educators will need to work not only on refining methods of presenting religious material, but will also need to be vigilant in clarifying the content of religious education.

Notes

1. Sherry Turkle, *The Second Self: Computers and the Human Spirit* (New York: Simon & Schuster, 1984).
2. Craig Brod, *Technostress* (Reading, Mass: Addison-Wesley, 1984), p.16.
3. Ibid., pp. 125-26.

4. Alexander King, "Introduction: A New Industrial Revolution or Just Another Technology?" in *Microelectronics and Society,* ed. Guenter Friedrichs and Adam Schaff (New York: New American Library, 1983), p. 20.
5. Alvin Toffler, *The Third Wave* (New York: William Morrow, 1980), p. 12.
6. Fritjof Capra, *The Turning Point* (New York: Simon & Schuster, 1982), p. 33.
7. Joseph Weizenbaum, *Computer Power and Human Reason* (San Francisco: W. H. Freedman, 1976), p. iv.
8. J. David Bolter, *Turning's Man* (Chapel Hill: University of North Carolina, 1984), p. 10.
9. Ibid., p. 11.
10. Lewis Mumford, *Technics and Civilization* (New York: Harcourt Brace Jovanovich, 1934), p. 3.
11. Ibid.
12. Clyde L. Manschreck, *A History of Christianity in the World* (Englewood Cliffs, N. J.: Prentice-Hall, 1974), p. 149.
13. Mumford, *Technics and Civilization,* p. 24.
14. Ibid., p. 34.
15. Ibid., p. 33.
16. Magali Sarfatti Larson, *The Rise of Professionalism* (Berkeley: University of California Press, 1977), p. xvii.
17. Ibid., p. 238.
18. John G. Kemeny, *Man and the Computer* (New York: Charles Schribner's Sons, 1972), pp. 3-5.

CHAPTER NINE

THE
FUTURE

I T is difficult to write about future developments in the use of computers for religious education, for two reasons. The first is the general unpredictability of the future role of computers—not only in education but in the whole society. Second, the field is developing so quickly that what is suggested as a future development may already have taken place or may have been tried and found unsuccessful.

But looking to the future is important. Decisions made about investing in religious education software or hardware should be informed by a sensitivity to likely developments. Chapters 3 and 4 discuss these specific issues. In addition, long-range planning is necessary. At both the local church and the denominational level, future use of computers and other technology depends largely upon the vision of religious educators today. The future of religious education will be what the church leaders make it.

Software

There is much need for serious software development. There were three stages in the development of software for church office use, and it appears that religious education software will follow the same pattern. In the first stage, individuals or small groups used tremendous creativity to produce surprisingly useful software products for offices. Some of the pioneers provided resources especially for churches. But the overall quality for both secular and church use was relatively low. Users needed to be committed to overcoming difficulties in order to make both the hardware and the software work properly.

During that stage, two or three people often worked together to produce software for church administration. They would write the manual, sell the software to churches, then help the churches learn to use it, while at the same time solving any problems. Exactly the same thing happened with business software.

Today, educational software is at this first stage. Much of the software being used in schools has been written by small teams of educators, and some very creative people have focused on providing religious education software. As a result, the quality of educational software for secular and religious use is similar. There are some excellent programs for schools, and several of the religious education programs are pioneering works—not only in religious education, but in the whole area of computer-assisted education.

The development of computers for administrative use by churches is now in its second stage. During this stage there has been tremendous expenditure of time and energy to produce computer software for the business community, and some of this software is being used by churches. These products have been developed by large teams of programmers. They are easier to use, less vulnerable to errors due to user confusion, very powerful, and less expensive than the software developed in the first stage. Some examples are the very powerful word-processing programs developed between 1983 and 1985. Other software programs, such as Framework, could be adapted for church work, but a certain amount of skill is required to use the software in a church administrative setting.

During this stage the church has fallen behind. Resources were not committed to producing church administrative software as sophisticated as Framework. The investment of hundreds of thousands of dollars in software development could not be supported by the forward-thinking and creative individuals who had provided the software for church administration in the first stage.

During this stage, church administrators have begun to understand what computers can do. Some churches eagerly started using software that had been developed in the first stage. Others have tried to use the same software the business community uses. This stage presents denominational officials with a dilemma: They see the difficulty of providing the necessary resources to produce software as sophisticated as commercial business software, but they are also convinced that churches need administrative resources.

Religious educators can expect a similar experience. Far more money will be available to secular educators, so that very high-quality software will be produced. This software will demonstrate that computers can be used effectively for education. Religious educators will be caught between the increasing awareness that computers can be a powerful tool for education, and the reality that to produce materials similar to those used in secular education would require time and money beyond the normal budgets of the curriculum-development departments of denominations.

It seems unlikely that the millions of dollars necessary for religious educators to produce quality software can (or should) be raised and spent. Over the next decade, we can expect that millions of dollars will be spent on the development of educational software. During this stage, religious education software will look very unsophisticated when compared to that used in schools.

But the third stage offers hope. During the third stage, the software developed for secular use will become so sophisticated that it can easily be adapted for church use. For church administration, this stage will probably begin before the end of the 1980s. For educational software, it will come a little later, depending upon how quickly stage two develops in the educational field.

In this third stage the software will not be restricted by the content of the material being processed by the computer. It will work equally well with church school attendance records or with warehouse inventories. And educational software will be equally adaptable: The same program could be used to teach physics or theology. This software will be developed after stage-two software has been developed and tested. The information gained from those experiments will determine the exact nature of this "general use" software. We can be certain that it will be very easy for both students and teachers to use.

Looking ahead to the third stage gives religious educators a clear way to strategize use of computers during this first stage. It is important to experiment with the religious education software developed as part of the first stage, and with the secular software developed as part of the second stage, because it will help the church focus on the issues that need to be addressed in the third stage. Thus, as the third stage develops, religious educators will be prepared to take full advantage of it.

Hardware

The sophistication of educational software in the future depends in part upon the availability of increasingly sophisticated hardware. All indications are that we can expect more powerful computers and decreasing prices. The changes in hardware are important primarily because of the implications that these changes have for software development. Five probable future developments are of particular importance: increased computing speed, increased internal memory, increased off-line storage, improved computer-to-computer communication, and new and improved input devices.

Today, when computers commonly process several million instructions per second, speed does not appear to be an issue. With today's educational software, when the computer asks a question and then only checks to compare that answer to one expected answer, the response appears to be instantaneous. But if tomorrow's educational software will compare an answer to a variety of possible answers, diagnose why the student answered in a particular way, and compare that answer to previous answers to search for an underlying pattern, then computers will need to be much faster. This might be accomplished in several ways. The time it takes the computer to go through each step could simply be decreased, or several computer processors could be used at the same time. The student would experience only one computer, but the work might be accomplished by several computers working together.

Computers of the near future will have much larger internal memory storage—the place where software and information are stored electronically—so that they are immediately available for processing. There probably will be technical advancements to make this storage less expensive, but increasing the amount of internal storage can also be simply a design decision, mandated by the requirements of future software.

Most educational software designed today does not require a large amount of off-line storage—the disk drive or other device where information is stored. But as educational software becomes more sophisticated, it will use much larger data bases, and this will require equipment with very rapid access to large amounts of off-line storage. We can expect that in the near future computers will be designed with this in mind. Disks called CD ROMS will probably prove to be a way to make great amounts of information available to a single user. A large library of information can be stored on a single CD ROM. A church might have a collection of disks, containing as much information as is now found in a college library.

At the present time most educational use of computers involves a student interacting with a single computer. But the future will see computers working together—one computer may look to another for expert advice. For example, a student using a particular computer to study Paul's second letter to Corinth might begin to wonder whether there were examples of similar letters written to people who participated in non-Christian cults in Corinth. The student asks the computer, but that information is not part of the software being used. Rather than responding that it cannot answer, the computer would contact another computer where bibliographies and indexes are stored. A list of resources would then be presented to the student.

The individual computers used by students might be connected to a master computer, which the teacher uses to evaluate progress and identify areas in which additional instruction is necessary. The students' computers would transmit information to the teacher's computer, where it would be combined with other information and analyzed. Some future advances in computer-to-computer communication will be in the area of improved software for this process. But we can also expect hardware that will make it possible for information to be transferred more rapidly and efficiently.

The typewriter keyboard is sometimes a deterent to achieving educational goals, because both children and adults may have difficulty typing. The ability of computers to understand spoken words is being perfected. Computers which can receive information that is spoken, rather than typed, will probably be available soon. Already available are devices that can read typed pages. Future developments will increase the opportunities for programmers of educational software to use a variety of methods for people-to-computer communication.

Computers and Video

The marriage of computers and video seems natural, but it is not clear exactly what the implications will be for religious education. Computers can be used to direct the presentation of material that has been prepared by using traditional video techniques, or they can simulate video presentations. Some video cassette recorders use a small computer to control the recording and playing back of taped television programs. In this situation, the computer determines the order of presentation of a series of visual images. But a computer can also create cartoon characters.

Advancements in video disk technology enable video equipment to store digital information, just as floppy disks do. But the video disk can also store video pictures or whole television scenes.

One could imagine a vast collection of video recordings of the Holy Land, controlled by a computer program, so that a student could explore the villages and countryside at will. Such a program could include information about climate and weather so that typical conditions would be included. Looking even farther into the future, one could imagine the computer enhancing or modifying the video images so that the student could see the scenes with appropriate lighting. A sunrise over the Sea of Galilee could be constructed by the computer from the video images available to it.

Creating the necessary software and collecting the video tapes for this type of presentation would be a monumental undertaking. It seems unlikely that churches will have the resources for projects of this nature in the foreseeable future. But video and computers can be used in more modest ways. This has been demonstrated in experiments with teaching particular skills. For example, video tapes are prepared showing the problems that can develop with a bicycle. Tapes are also made showing how to solve each problem. The computer presents the portions of the tapes requested by a student. If one step is not fully understood, it can be viewed repeatedly. Additional instructions or a closeup view of a particularly difficult step can be provided. A student can guide the computer to present the necessary information so that a problem with a bicycle can be diagnosed and repaired.

In religious education, a computer could present a video scene on a screen. This could be discussed by a class and a series of questions answered. The computer might use the answers to display a new scene, to help the class focus on the specific issues raised in the discussion.

Artificial Intelligence

Developments in the field of artificial intelligence may have a great impact on future developments in the educational use of computers. It does not matter whether scientists finally decide that intelligence is something that can be transferred to a machine. The research being conducted into the nature of knowledge and understanding, the methods of communicating knowledge, and the process of exercising judgment, will result in improved educational theory and changing educational practices. Because the results of artificial-intelligence research include improvement in understanding how computers can be used, we can expect advancements in understanding how they can be used for education. As Parker Rossman points out in *Computers: Bridges to the Future*, "The promise of 'artificial intelligence' research lies in what it teaches us about ourselves, and about the brains that create computers, so that we can create 'intellectual tools' to do things we have never done before."[1]

The ultimate goal of the artificial-intelligence movement has not changed since it was defined by Alan Turing in the 1930s. He said that we could consider a machine to be intelligent if, when it was placed at the other end of a telephone line and we conversed with it, we could not tell whether we were talking to a human or to a machine. Such a machine needs to respond to our subtle meanings. And it must be able to learn from our conversation. The interpretation of language and the theory of learning are the basis for artificial intelligence research in the mid-1980s. This research would be of interest to educators, even if it could not be implemented on computers.

One of the thrusts of artificial-intelligence research is the development of expert systems—hardware-software systems with large collections of information which can be used to respond to new situations. This approach depends on the development of very powerful computers which can process large amounts of information. Even if expert systems do not prove to be capable of mimicking intelligent behavior, they certainly can be used for some tasks that do not require the powers of intelligence. In this way, humans can be freed to concentrate on tasks which do require intelligence.

A popular early experiment resulted in a computer program called "Eliza." This program has been converted to a simplified form for use on personal computers and provides a sense of what it might mean if artificial intelligence is created. The program makes a computer respond as if it were a psychologist. Below is a sample printout produced by the program. User input is printed in upper case; the computer's responses are in lower case.

to have the question repeated just press a <cr>;
to end the session just tell eliza to "shut up."
*important—you must use upper case for all your answers.
hit any key to continue.
hi! i am eliza. what is your problem?
I AM VERY TIRED
do you like being tired?
NO
can you say more about that?
I NEED MORE SLEEP
i see
THAT WAS A DUMB ANSWER
do you wish you were a dumb answer?
NO I HATE COMPUTERS
are you talking about me in particular?
YES
come, come, elucidate your thoughts.
SHUT UP

Responding to a computer as if it were intelligent is an unnerving experience. James Eastman, in reviewing the "Eliza" program, observed that it teaches us how unintelligent are most of the conversations in which we participate. If a very simple computer program can do as well as we often do when we communicate with each other, what does that say about the level of our communication? The same question can be raised about our teaching. If a computer can mimic most of what we do in the classroom, what does that say about the quality of our teaching? Possibly the most important contribution religious education will receive from the study of artificial intelligence is that it challenges us to use our human intelligence more fully.

Notes

1. Parker Rossman, *Computers: Bridges to the Future* (Valley Forge, Penna.: Judson Press, 1985), p. 12.

T HE following list of religious education software was prepared by Dr. James Eastman in April of 1985. A current list may be obtained by writing: Dr. James Eastman, Manager, Churchwide EDP, Presbyterian Church (U.S.A.), 475 Riverside Dr., Rm. 1908, New York NY 10115. Dr. Eastman would also be pleased to hear from readers about new products.

* * *

American Baptist Churches
Literature Services
P.O. Box 851
Valley Forge PA 19482-0851

Roger Price, coordinator of computer education in the Division of Church Education, American Baptist Churches, has produced three booklets containing BASIC programs for church education. The user enters the program (i.e., types in the BASIC codes).

When ordering, give both number and title. $1.95 each, plus postage and handling.

The Ten Commandments—A Learning Game from the Bible (LS 12-301)

Bible Knowledge—A Learning Game from the Bible (LS 12-302)

Life Choices—A Life Simulation Game (LS 12-303)

Baker Book House
P.O. Box 6287
Grand Rapids MI 49506

Software is available for the Apple II Plus, IIe, IIc, and Commodore 64. Each disk has fifteen stories for children ages 8–13. The stories involve the "Baker Street Kids," who dress up and act out Bible stories. Each story is followed by questions. $29.95.

* * *

Bible Research Systems
9415 Burnet Rd.
Austin TX 78758

This company has the entire King James Version of the Bible on computer diskettes, available for Apple II, most MS-DOS computers, most CP/M computers, and the Radio Shack TRS-80 Model III and IV. The user searches the text, using key words appropriate to a topic.

* * *

The C-4 Computer Company
115 Neil St., P.O. Box 1408
Champaign IL 61820

Adam Christian Education Programs have been designed to run on the Apple II Plus, Apple IIe, and Apple III. These programs can be used with an unlimited number of players and will keep scores and records for up to 10 players. The programs currently available:

"Overview of the Bible No. 1"—teaches the user to identify the major theme of each book in the Bible.

"Overview of the Bible No. 2"—contains the biblical overview.

"Overview of the Bible No. 3"—focuses attention on the major biblical leaders.

The company has several additional programs:

"Bible Games"; "The Travels of Paul"; "The Sermon on the Mount"; "The Teachings of Jesus"; "Ralph's Bible Games."

Christian Computer/Based Communications
44 Delma Dr.
Toronto, Ontario M8W 4N6

This company has a variety of tutorial programs and games that run on Commodore equipment. The company also serves as a clearing house for Christian programs for various Commodore computers.

* * *

Christian Software/CJRJ Enterprises
301 S. Purdue
Claremore OK 74017

The program **"Books of the Bible"** comes in both tape and disk form for the Commodore 64. **"Hymns of the Faith"** is a disk for the Commodore 64, with 25 hymns in 3-part harmony, plus words to all verses. $14.95 each.

Christian Software also sells three Game Packs for the Radio Shack Color Computer with 16K extended BASIC. $44.95 each.

* * *

Church School Software
601 W. Highway 83
Bensenville IL 60106

This company has the following products for the TIMEX/Sinclair 1000/1500:

"What Cross Is This?"—Same or different? (kindergarten)

"What Cross Is This?"—Which one matches? (grades 1, 2)

"What Cross Is This?"—What is my name? (grades 3, 4)

"What Cross Is This?"—Identify from description (grade 5 to adult)

"Bible Words" (grades 1–3)

"Let Me Guess" (grades 1–3)

"Which Disciple?" (grade 4 to adult)

"Bible Books" (grades 4–8)

"Two Sons"—the prodigal son story, role-played by 1 to 3 persons (grade 5 to adult)

"What Shall I Do?"—students choose between attending two very important events (grade 6 to high school)

"Let's Write a Prayer" (grade 4 to adult)

"Using the Hymnal" (grade 5 to adult)

"Bible Quiz"—teachers can prepare multiple choice questions with own curriculum content (grade 3 to adult)

"Ten Commandments Drill" (grades 4–8)

"Modern Psalmist"—'hymnwriter' provides an aid for composing new words to familiar melodies (grade 7 to adult)

"Plan a Worship Service" (grade 7 to adult)

"Bible Bingo" (grade 3 to adult)

Programs on tape are $6 each and include a listing of the program. Listing only in generic BASIC—$3.00.

* * *

CompuBible
P.O. Box 685
Borger TX 79008

A computerized Bible permits study of up to five different subjects at one time. The screen can be divided into windows so two passages may be compared. Complete Bible with program disks—$299.

* * *

Cross Educational Software
1802 N. Trenton St.
P.O. Box 1536
Ruston LA 71270

This company sells a line of teacher aids, including material for physics and chemistry courses. A product called **"Create-A-Test"** allows a teacher to select questions for a test and could be used in Christian education.

They also have the following products designed specifically for Christian education:

Presbyterian—Catechism, Bible Books, Hymns
Methodist—Bible Books, Hymns
The hymn programs include sound, the words of the hymn, and a ball that bounces over the words. The other programs include graphic displays.

"Super Sampson" (Apple II) $15.00
"Bible Books" (Apple II, IBM-PC, Commodore 64) $15.00
"Caroling" (Apple II, IBM-PC) $15.00

* * *

Davka Corporation
845 N. Michigan Ave., Suite 843
Chicago IL 60611

Bible stories combined with video action:
"Sampson & Delilah" (Apple II Plus and IIe; Commodore 64) $24.95
"Jericho" (Apple II Plus and IIe; Atari models with 48K) $24.95
"The Philistine Play" (Apple II Plus and IIe) $34.95
"The Lion's Share" (Apple II Plus and IIe) $34.95

* * *

GRAPE
P.O. Box 576
Keyport WA 98366

Gospel Resource and Program Exchange publishes six issues of the *GRAPE Vine* a year. The newsletter serves as a clearing house for Christian programs for the Apple computer and costs $5.00 per year.

* * *

Institute of Church Ministry
Andrews University
Berrien Springs MI 49104

Bible Word Games—four computer-facilitated Bible games, based on a list of over 400 names of Bible characters and places: **"Memory," "Anagrams,"**

"**Search,**" "**Challenge.**" Each has three levels of play. (IBM-PC version, $31.95; Apple II version, $24.95)

"**Bible Verse Cipher**"—an interactive computer game to decipher a selected Bible verse chosen at random from almost 300 verses; three levels of difficulty (IBM-PC) $24.95

This company offers volume discounts, beginning with six units.

* * *

Linguist's Software
P.O. Box 231
Mt. Hermon CA 95041

Products for the Apple MacIntosh transform the keyboard into either the Greek or Hebrew alphabet. A program called "**Phonetics**" produces the symbols of the phonetic alphabet, plus 22 additional symbols.

"**Mac Greek**"—$119; "**Mac Hebrew**"—$119.

"**Mac Greek,**" "**Mac Hebrew,**" *and* "**Phonetics**"— $199.95.

* * *

Little David Enterprises, Inc.
P.O. Box 91
Fairless Hills PA 19030

"**Knowledge Bible**"—for 2 to 10 players; tests knowledge of the King James Bible (Commodore 64 with a single 1541 or compatible disk drive) $29.95.

* * *

Magic Ministry
Zion Lutheran Church
Dauphin PA 17018

Six packages for the Commodore 64:

"**Mark**"—multiple-choice questions lead the user on a chapter-by-chapter journey (also available in Apple-soft)

"**Luke**"—similar to above.

"**Acts**"—based on the Acts of the Apostles. When questions are answered correctly, churches are established on a map of the area Paul visited.

"**Books**"—an aid in memorizing books of the Bible.

"**Confirmation Exams**"—true/false exams rewritten from the Lutheran *Catechetics for Today*.

"**Law**"—review and quiz on Martin Luther's explanation of the Ten Commandments. One program, $20; any 2 programs, $35; any 3, $50; any 4, $60; any 5, $70. "**Law**" is free with any other program.

* * *

Omega Software
P.O. Box 355
Round Rock TX 78680

Four versions of the Bible—King James Version, New International Version, New King James Version, The Living Bible:

"**The Scripture Scanner**"—helps create lessons plans, study guides, and research outlines; uses windows for comparative study of text on screen (IBM PC and compatibles). Complete Bible—$249.95.

* * *

RTS Outreach
5829 Little Mountain Dr.
Ellenwood GA 30049

"**Fisherman Game**"—teaches those 8 and older Bible facts and values; includes more than 2,000 questions (IBM PC and compatibles). $39.95

* * *

Scripture Software
P.O. Bos 6131-C
Orlando FL 32853

A Bible search program; King James Version with words in italics enclosed in brackets (TRS-80). $225.

SEI Enterprises, Inc.
17 Serpi Rd.
Highland Mills NY 10930

"Seek-Bible"—2 to 10 players, using their own King James Bibles, conduct searches, competing with one another and the clock (Commodore 64 and VIC-20 with 16 K expansion). Cassette, $24.95; disk, $29.95

"Bible-Grams"—2 to 10 players, using their King James Bibles, compete in solving Bible anagrams. Computers and prices same as above.

* * *

Smoky Mountain Software
13 Catatoga Path
Brevard NC 28712

Programs for the Commodore:

"Sort 'em 1—Creation/Flood/Baby Moses"—player sorts set of illustrations into proper order (age 5 and up). Disk—$24.95

"Sort 'em 2—Garden/Joseph/Bush"—second in series.

"Scrambled Verses"—player unscrambles text; running score and clock are displayed at bottom of screen. Disk—$29.95

"Hidden Words"—generates any number of different word-search puzzles from words supplied by player; uses printer to put puzzles and answer key on paper. Disk—$19.95

"Bible Trip"—adventure game on New Testament geography. Disk—$19.95

"Bible Mates"—a drill; match spouses in the Bible. Disk—$14.95

"New Testament Jobs"—player uses knowledge of New Testament jobs to win chariot race. Disk—$14.95

"Old Testament Jobs"—player used knowledge of Old Testament jobs to win sailboat race. Disk—$14.95

"Old Testament Guess Who"—match Old Testament people with clues supplied. Disk—$14.95

"**Gospels Guess Who**"—same as above, for Matthew, Mark, Luke, John. Disk— $14.95

"**Acts Guess Who**"—same as above, for Acts. Disk— $14.95

"**Books of the Bible**"—drill; order of the books of the Bible. Disk—$14.95

* * *

Theobyte
8163 Fayette
Kansas City KS 66109

An electronic concordance that will survey a whole disk, search for up to 6 words, create vocabulary lists for Bible passages, and convert modern spelling of New Testament names to the King James equivalent. Program disk—$6.00; disk and New Testament texts—$54.00

* * *

The United Presbyterian Church in the U.S.A.
Curriculum Services UPCUSA
925 Chestnut St.
Philadelphia PA 19107

Five programs written by David Wasserman and Mark Russell come in a single package (Apple II, Commodore 64, IBM PC and compatibles, and Kaypro-CP/M) $29.95 each:

"**Background Essay**"

"**Jesus Is Born**"—multiple-choice questions

"**People and Places**"—matching game

"**The Birth Stories**"—multiple-choice questions with discussion starters

"**What Do You Think?**"—players respond to a series of opinion-seeking questions; results are tabulated and can be used as discussion starters.

* * *

Word of God
88 Long Court
Thousand Oaks CA 91360

The King James Bible, Strong's *Concordance*, Greek and Hebrew dictionaries—all integrated into one package containing 10 study functions.

CD ROM
A compact-disk player which is connected to a computer to use information that has been stored on compact disks.

central processing unit
The part of the computer in which the actual manipulation of electronic symbols takes place.

chip
The core of the central processing unit.

compatible
Software or hardware that can be used on machines manufactured by different companies.

database management software
Software that organizes information about items or individuals into records. Many database managers can work with more than one set of records at a time.

file
A collection of records, all containing the same categories of information.

floppy-disk drive
An off-line storage device which uses removable plastic disks to store programs or information.

graphics

Computer graphics use the symbol-manipulating capabilities of computers to create patterns on a screen or on paper. Computer symbols are interpreted by the computer to place small dots on a paper or screen. Cartoon-like figures are one example.

hard-disk drive

An off-line storage device which stores large amounts of information and transfers information to the computer very quickly.

hardware

The computer equipment.

joy stick

An input device—a small rod protruding from a base. When the rod is rotated, the computer receives signals interpreted as directions to move objects on the screen.

keyboard

A device which looks like a typewriter, used to enter information into a computer.

light pen

Pencil-like device which can be pointed at the computer screen to input information.

modem

A device used to convert computer signals into electronic pulses which can be transmitted over telephone wires. The modem also converts pulses received over the phone line into signals a computer can interpret.

mouse

An input device which is rolled on the table to indicate that objects on the computer screen should be moved.

monitor

A television-like screen used to display computer output.

off-line storage
Any one of a number of hardware devices used to store software or data during the execution of programs or when the computer is turned off.

operating system
The software which controls the elementary functions of the computer, such as keyboard entry and disk organization. Common operating systems are MS-DOS and CP/M.

printer
An output device which produces printed copy on paper.

program
Program is another name for an item of *software*.

record
The information kept about one item or individual in a database.

software
The set of instructions which controls the operation of the computer. Software is usually sold on a disk, which is then inserted into the computer disk drive.

spreadsheet
A software program which organizes information into rows and columns.

telecommunication
The use of computers to send information from one place to another.

touch screens
Specially designed computer systems which accept information by noting where the monitor screen has been touched.